PRAISE FOR *REVENGE OF THE JILTED DRAPERIES*

"Maralys Wills' new collection of stories is so much fun! Each one is different—some reflective and serious, others humorous—but they are all entertaining. I found myself so amused as I carried on that I was glad I wasn't reading them in public. The funniest one for me was the title story, "Revenge of the Jilted Draperies." I had tears rolling down my face, and I couldn't read it out loud to my husband because I was laughing so hard I was unintelligible."

IRENE BERARDESCO, B.A.

"Maralys Wills—she of *Higher than Eagles* and *Damn the Rejections, Full Speed Ahead* fame—has done it again. She charms her way into our hearts and right down to our funny bones with whimsical musings that will rip at your heart strings or make you laugh out loud."

JAN MURRA, Author, *Castoff*

"Maralys' stories are always current and relevant to life today. She injects humor, wisdom, and honesty—and her writing style keeps me interested and wanting more."

MOLLY NUNN

REVENGE OF THE JILTED DRAPERIES

And Other
Sweet-and-Sour Stories

Also by Maralys Wills

The Tail on my Mother's Kite

So You're Seventy ... So What?

*Buy a Trumpet and Blow Your Own Horn:
Turning Books into Bucks*

*Damn the Rejections, Full Speed Ahead:
The Bumpy Road to Getting Published*

A Clown in the Trunk: A Memoir

A Circus Without Elephants: A Memoir

Save My Son

Scatterpath: A Thriller

*Higher Than Eagles: The Tragedy and Triumph
of an American Family*

Fun Games for Great Parties

Soar and Surrender

A Match for Always

Mountain Spell

Tempest and Tenderness

Man Birds: Hang Gliders & Hang Gliding

Revenge of the Jilted Draperies

And Other Sweet-and-Sour Stories

MARALYS WILLS

LEMON LANE PRESS • SANTA ANA, CALIFORNIA

Cover and Book Design: Sue Campbell

ISBN: 978-0-9961675-3-6 (print book)
ISBN: 978-0-9961675-4-3 (e-book)

Contact Lemon Lane Press:
(714) 544-0445
or the author: Maralys@Cox.net
Lemon Lane Press
1811 Beverly Glen Dr.
Santa Ana, California 92705

Printed in the United States of America

Dedicated to all the fascinating people, family and otherwise, who provide me with stories.

CONTENTS

The Perils of Popcorn

My husband, Rob, has a thing about burning down the house. "Don't start the dryer at bedtime, Babe. I don't want to smell smoke in the middle of the night." "Don't leave the kitchen while the oven's on. The house could catch fire."

Apparently he wants me right there, watching, when flames start licking out of the appliances.

Clearly Rob has given no thought to what else might happen in a house. One evening, two weeks ago, he stuck a bag of popcorn in the microwave and set the timer in the dark. Exempt from his own don't-leave-the-oven rule, he returned to his family room chair.

Soon I began smelling a smell. Not a good smell. Tentatively, I peeked into the microwave, and quickly slammed it shut. Smoke had already collected into a black, stampeding ball, just waiting for some fool to let it out. "The popcorn's burned!" I shouted toward his chair. "The microwave is full of smoke. I don't dare open the door!"

"Just wait, Babe," he said calmly. "It'll go away." Well, he was right. Some of the smoke escaped without anyone's help. Out through seams and cracks that only a science fiction demon could find. Our kitchen took on a sinister cast. This was no ordinary smoke—it was the same chemical effluvium that seeps out of dangerous, futuristic labs, for which daffy scientists scramble for gas masks.

Mask-free, I ran around the family room and front hall, opening outside doors, then propping them open. The cats were bewildered. *She's letting us come and go—at will?* I turned on the attic fan in the hall, which sucks in air from outside. I switched on the fan over the stove.

Nothing helped. The foul air grew worse and crept over to Rob's chair.

He said, "You'd better remove the popcorn. Grab it quick and throw it outside." He made it sound easy, but the job actually required preparation. First I ran to the back door, sucked in a lungful of clean air and, holding my breath, I darted to the microwave, seized the popcorn, and flung it outside toward the garage. Eventually I allowed myself another real breath. But not in the kitchen.

The atmosphere in our kitchen and family room was now toxic. Unless you stood in an outside doorway, breathing seemed a dangerous option. Inevitably, a question occurred to me: *WHAT did they put in the popcorn?* I said to Rob, "Surely, you'll never eat *that* stuff again!" And Rob, who would set down a heavy sack of groceries to retrieve a dime in the gutter, said, "Well, there's only one more bag," implying that even one bag of poison was worth saving.

We could only escape the fumes by going to bed.

The next day the two rooms were still alive with odor. A rag dipped in Pinesol and swabbed around the microwave's interior removed a horrible, yellowish layer of scum, but in no way interrupted the smell. A second swabbing was equally useless. Some odors simply can't be overcome. We'd have done as well with the residue from a skunk.

At last, one week later, the kitchen air was once again breathable. But not near the microwave. Our appliance might have survived its ill-fated encounter with popcorn, but now it had putrid pores and bad breath. And areas of noxious vapors still lurked in the family room.

"I'm through with this disgusting thing," I said to Rob, and to my surprise, he didn't argue. Instead, he gamely carried it out to the curb—and propped up a sign that said, "Free. It Works." The truth never made the sign. "Permanent Stench."

Before evening, old stinky-pooh was gone.

But my mental images weren't. I could almost see the astonished look of the new owner as she fired it up … could almost hear her words. "Oh, my God, Harry, where did you get this awful-smelling object? Take it to the curb. Quick!"

Well, afterwards I had a word or two for Rob. "You don't have to burn down a house to destroy it, you know. You can always just stink it to death!"

The Eternal Cookie Sheet

NOTHING IS FOREVER, BUT SOME THINGS COME close. I'm speaking of a group my husband and I assembled forty-seven years ago to discuss current events. Rob and I were young then—and so were all the other couples. These days Discussion Group itself is at times creaky, albeit with flashes of youthful vigor. But happily, it lives on.

Now, all these years later, various couples have moved away or well … died. We may be the only originals left. But our kids and our friends' kids have joined, so the group has an everlasting quality—a multi-generational thing. Each month the topic resonates with some and bores others, but about one thing we're unanimous—we all love the potluck.

Yet there's this about potlucks—when you bring food to someone's house, you're bound to forget something: a hot pot holder, a serving spoon, a packet of croûtons, an outdoor jacket. My potholder drawer is full of unfamiliar squares of cloth, my hall closet wraps its arms around two strange jackets, and for years my best serving spoon—large, good-looking, and sturdy—has been missing. I keep looking for it at other people's homes, but I think I must have left it with someone who died.

Four months ago—the last time we were hosts—a couple left a cookie sheet. It was old and rusty, ownership unknown. And frankly, in an attempt to discover its natural home, I wasn't about to make fourteen phone calls. But next morning my friend Micki called. "Yes," I said, "I found the cookie sheet."

She lives a fair distance, which explains why she said, "I'll come get it in a few days—when I'm down your way. Just put it on the front porch."

For a month and a half, along with a pot of flowers, the rusty cookie sheet hovered near our front door. Nobody ever asked, "Why is a cookie sheet living on your porch?" Maybe we were assumed to be a little odd.

At the next Discussion Group, I remembered to bring it along. But that month the couple didn't come.

The following month, at which the couple DID appear, I forgot to put the thing in my car.

At last, this month, the cookie-sheet couple moved into hosting position. Three weeks ago, Rob said, "For God's sake, Babe, put that damn cookie sheet in your car." So I stuck it in back, where for weeks it bumped the legs of whoever was riding with us.

Last night, at 2:00 a.m., Rob gave a final order. "Move the cookie sheet to the dashboard. Now. Or we'll forget it again."

I said sourly, "It's 2:00 a.m. The spiders are out. I'll

move it in the morning."

"You'll forget," he said.

"I'll put a note over the stove." All night the note dangled there, waiting to be released to the waste basket. Meanwhile the kitchenware rested peacefully in its backseat home.

I swore to myself, *If I forget it tonight, I'll make a special trip and drive the damn thing back to its owner. And I don't care how far away she lives.* I suddenly saw a limit to playing gracious hostess to a tarnished cookie sheet.

But that night my memory and Rob's memory kicked in, for once in unison, and together we returned it home.

The owner stared in surprise. "I forgot all about it." She took a closer look. "It looks kind of used up, doesn't it? Maybe I'll just throw it away."

I nodded without speaking. *I should have done that four months ago.*

But while I was there, I rummaged through her kitchen drawers for my serving spoon. No luck. I guess I really DID leave it with someone who's now in heaven. With the way this is going, she took the spoon with her.

A DEVILISH DESIGN

IT CAME TO ME TODAY THAT DESIGNING A COM-
mercial product requires a certain kind of genius: an
inner vision of the never-before-seen, combined with
a yearning for simplicity. I recall with amazement those
few products that reached a large market, but lacked the
essentials ... that were seemingly created by idiots.

Take my earliest stove tops, for instance. Suddenly
this morning I saw a link between a succession of stoves,
the door on a Lincoln Town Car, and a disastrous pair
of tennis shoes—all suffering from unimaginable design
flaws.

The earliest of these products was a ridiculous stove
top. In order to remove the parts for cleaning, you had
to use a screwdriver to take out a few screws, or in later
versions, unwind certain parts, or shift two or three levers ... in essence do a dismantling job reminiscent of
replacing the transmission on a car.

The first designers apparently thought that without
all these nuts and bolts, parts of the stove might come
apart and ... do what? Fall off the counter? Blow away?
The flaws persisted through several permutations and
various brand names—until some simplicity-oriented
inventor finally figured out that gravity alone, plus a few

well-placed grooves, would hold everything in place.

I recall my delight when I finally bought a stove top for which all the parts merely lifted off. No screws, no bolts, no levers. And sure enough, gravity did its job.

The Lincoln Town Car, a decade ago, embodied the height of freakish design. I hadn't had my new/used Lincoln long before the enormous driver's door, curved inward like a scimitar, took a chunk out of my left leg. You couldn't close that door and simultaneously get out of its way. The second time this happened, I stared down at my bloody leg in horror. Next day I limped to the dealership and sold the car. I decided my calf couldn't survive one more mean-spirited bite from the Lincoln … whose engineers had somehow managed to combine a luxury car with elements of a Rottweiler.

Only a few days later, four of us were discussing our brief and dangerous encounters with this high-end vehicle. All four of us had suffered significant leg gashes before offloading our lethal Lincolns. This flaw never achieved media attention but, in the manner of gossip, was damned quietly among its users.

The last design flaw could have killed me. My new tennis shoes, supposedly designed with ergonomic inner springs, were so thick, top to bottom, and so unstable, that occasionally I found myself lurching forward, tripped up by my own footwear.

I should have tossed away the shoes. But hey, they

were new, so I didn't. What happened next was so trau-matic that I can't bring myself, at the moment, to relate the details. Suffice it to say that two doctors informed me one evening that these spectacular athletic shoes had caused a number of noteworthy accidents.

My next story describes how a pair of poorly-de-signed shoes launched me into space—something like Sputnik. And speaking of space—with their propensity for design errors, how did American engineers succeed in putting men on the moon? Instead of, say ... Venus?

Sailing Into Space—Without Wings

I couldn't have predicted this crazy accident.

One late afternoon, as I bent over to retrieve theater tickets off the front porch, the inexplicable happened. When I tried to rise, my feet were everywhere—except under me.

Whether it was my new, extra-fat tennis shoes or a simple loss of balance, I couldn't tell. I was only aware that I found myself lurching, pedaling, and slapping at the Palos Verdes rock as I tried to regain my feet. And not succeeding.

Instead, all that fancy foot work launched me off the porch and out over our two front steps. Literally into space.

I was airborne long enough to realize there was no soft landing in sight, that cement was everywhere and I would inevitably hit our inlaid-stone walkway. Horrified as I sailed, I came down from an exaggerated altitude and smacked hard onto the stones.

For seconds I lay sprawled, unable to move. It hurt to breathe. But I was alive. I was conscious. And I hadn't hit my head.

I could see my right wrist was torn up, and God knows what else. From my ungainly splat on the walkway,

I yelled through the still-open front door, trying to attract my husband.

He didn't seem to hear. Which was nothing new.

Struggling to sit up, I could see him across the family room, calmly watching television. "Rob!" I screamed. "Rob! Help!"

He paid no attention, seemed riveted to the TV.

"Rob!" I screamed even louder, "Rob! Rob! Rob! Help!" Some part of me wondered how, for an injured person, I'd managed to yell so loud.

At last he stirred, as though awakening from a dream.

"Babe?" He leaned forward. "Where are you?"

"Help me!"

"What?" He pulled himself to his feet, ambled out to the porch. "What happened? What are you doing down there?"

Taking a nap. "I fell." A shallow, painful breath. "Off the porch." Another breath. "I've been yelling."

"Jesus, that was you? I thought it was the television. They were showing the Challenger coming apart. People were screaming on TV."

He now stood over me, baffled. "I finally realized it wasn't all television—it was you. Where are you hurt?"

"I don't know. Everywhere."

He reached down a hand. "Can you get up? If I help?"

"No."

"I'm not sure I can lift you, Babe. You'd be a dead weight." He thought a moment. "I'll call Chris. Maybe he's home." He looked down at me again. "Good God, look at your wrist."

"I know. It's a mess. I'm probably a mess in other places."

"I'll go call."

Chris was our son, an orthopedic surgeon who lived half a mile away. Rob disappeared and was back in minutes. "He just got home, Babe. He'll be right down."

I nodded, instantly relieved. I was alive. And Chris was coming. For the moment nothing else mattered.

CHRIS IS ONE OF THOSE DOCTORS WHO MAKES YOU feel better simply by showing up. That goes for his wife, too.

They arrived together, Betty-Jo with a warm look of sympathy, Chris with his usual aura of concern, almost a smile. The smile, or near smile, is reserved for non-emergencies. I was breathing, talking, clearly not a life or death case.

Chris looked me over, felt my ribs.

"Ouch! Ouch!"

"May be broken. We have to get you up." He turned to his dad. "Still got that walker—the one with a seat?"

Rob said he did, and minutes later, Betty-Jo, Chris,

and Rob eased me up onto the seat and pulled me up the two steps and into the family room. I explained what had happened.

With a gentle touch, Chris once more probed my ribs. "Well, Mom," he said cheerily, "they're probably broken, but even if they are, it won't make any difference. We don't do anything. Just let them heal on their own." He grinned. "Don't try to lift any pianos."

All I could do was nod.

The next day at his office, Chris pointed to x-rays that showed my ribs were intact. He turned to me with a look of satisfaction. "Good thing, Mom … you and I have the bones of dinosaurs. We don't break easily." He thought about it. "I'd send back the shoes. You don't need a second bite from the same dog."

So I did, describing in my note a certain relief that I hadn't been killed. Though clearly not new, the "trick" shoes brought a full refund. I suspect I wasn't the first customer who unwittingly soared away toward heaven, thanks to extra-powerful shoes with ergonomic springs.

A Strange Place For Drama

You never know what will happen at the post office.

Often in a slow line I've struck up conversations—with both men and women—and ended up giving them my card, or sometimes even a book. Or I've stood there doing a crossword puzzle and had the person next to me lean closer and say, "Five down is aloe."

"Oh, thanks," I say, and I'm thinking, *Hey, we're stuck here together, we might as well get acquainted!*

Post office stories come in good and bad flavors. The really bad ones were the times a knot of protesters camped just outside the door … two or three men with a card table and signs in big black letters, "Impeach Obama!" Underneath, hanging from the table, were photos of the president defiled by a Hitler mustache.

Often as I left I yelled over my shoulder, "Get lost!" What I wanted to do, actually, was push them into the gutter.

One day a bizarre thing happened. Several customers ahead of me, a husky man in a wheel chair got into a wrangle with the clerk behind the counter. He wheeled himself closer, and his chair just happened to hit the little metal stanchion that holds one end of the divider rope. In a sudden fit of anger, he grabbed the metal pole and slammed it to the ground. But the pole bounced back, so he seized it again and slammed it down harder. I stared at him, amazed. Others stared too, but nobody said anything.

Inspired by his own rage, the man picked up the stanchion with added fury, bent on crushing it once and for all. Without thinking, I yelled, "Cut it out! CUT IT OUT!" *Somebody* had to say *something*. With others around me simply murmuring, he finished his last slam and quit.

I couldn't believe my voice had been the only one. Eventually the man wheeled himself closer to the clerk, but he wasn't finished. Reaching above his head, he slammed his money onto the counter—with such a bang you could hear it reverberate throughout the post office. I left, wondering how much violence it would take before someone with testosterone stepped up and brought him to a halt.

Come to think of it, I think we were all struck dumb—like those first passengers on the 9-11 planes.

Today was the strangest post office day yet.

With twelve books to ship, I couldn't pack them at home—I needed one of the postal service's big priority boxes.

In a hurry to get there, I made a swift decision to wear, one last time, a sweat shirt I'd been on the point of giving away. It was twenty-three years old, which I happen to know because the good-looking insignia was right there on the shoulder—Queen Elizabeth Two—and it dated back to our fortieth anniversary, celebrated on that glorious ship. The shirt was a flashy mix of white and bright red, and even incorporated a few red and white stripes—vivid enough to make an impression on someone across the street.

Who knows what difference clothes can make?

As I was standing at the customer table, carefully packing books, a lovely-looking lady broke out of line and asked, "What are those books?"

"Memoirs," I said. And then added, "I wrote them."

"You wrote them?"

"Yes, it's my tenth book." I went on packing. "A story about our family."

Around her, people were starting to lean closer.

"Really," she said. "I work with older people, all of whom have great stories to tell. How did you get this published?"

I named the publisher, and she said, "That's the kind of thing we need to know."

When she paused I said, "I teach novel writing. Here, I'll give you my card." As I wrestled it out of my purse, to my surprise the man ahead of her in line put out his hand. "I'd like one."

I smiled at him. *Well, this is interesting!* I dug a little deeper, pulled out another card. And right then the lady in front of him said, "I'd like one, too."

Now I was *really* surprised! It was as though I'd suddenly been recognized as a celebrity ... Janet Evanovich come to Tustin. Immediately others spoke up, until almost everyone in line wanted cards, and I found my supply nearly depleted. Here I was, passing out six or seven cards to total strangers. I was laughing, thinking, *how did this happen?*

I said to the original lady, "Tell you what. I'll get you a book from my car."

"I'll watch your box," she said.

As I backed away toward the front of the line, everyone was looking at me and smiling, so I said for them all to hear, "I guess I should give a speech," and the whole group burst out laughing. *Well, I could,* I thought, *now that I've got the entire post office involved.*

Back at the car I decided, *What the hell, I might as well bring in two books.* Which I did. The first I gave to the original lady. And since the man was next in line, I hesitated, then handed him one, too. The room had taken on the atmosphere of a party.

Further down the line a lady said, "I'll BUY one!" So I gave her a card.

Once back in line with my books, I could see the man ahead of me already reading what I'd given him and smiling. As I reached the counter, the first woman rushed back inside and gave me her card.

Just before I handed over the big box, the lady who said she'd buy a book came up to talk, and we learned we were practically neighbors. "I'll be in touch," she said.

The clerk was smiling as I reached him. "Did you see what just happened?" I asked, and he nodded, as if to say, *Another post office drama.*

Home again, I studied myself in the mirror. *Was it me or this shirt from a famous passenger ship?* Impossible to be sure … except the garment had suddenly become a keeper. Just in case, I'll wear it in other settings. *Who knows what adventures I may yet experience with my friend, Queen Elizabeth?*

Pretty Boy Takes Wing

THE CATS WERE MY DAUGHTER'S IDEA. SHE KEPT saying to us, "Mom, you're upstairs writing day and night, and Dad's downstairs with nobody. He needs a cat for his lap."

Rob, being Rob, never agreed that his own company equaled nobody. For years, raised as an only child, he's been fully at ease with a state of aloneness. On the other hand, he's always preferred cats to at least half the human population—and I certainly like cats well enough, though I generally veer toward creatures that speak.

Anyway, under continuous pressure from Tracy, we visited a green-spirited animal shelter and brought home two black and white kittens. They were brothers and, as we soon learned, even related cats come with distinctive personalities.

As they grew, we discovered Bruiser was smart enough to pry open every sliding door in the house—at which point he followed us into room after room, settling down into nearby chairs. But he wasn't into physical affection, and when we tried to pet him, he ducked. He preferred our company at a distance.

Pretty Boy, on the other hand, was smart enough to learn that Rob's lap was a nice place for an evening's nap.

Exactly as Tracy had hoped.

By the time they were grown, somebody had given us a huge cat tower, which, as it turned out, was rickety. One day, with two cats aloft, the thing came apart and fell over. Both cats flew away from the spot as though from a roadside IED. Rob repaired it, but Bruiser never went near it again. Only Pretty Boy agreed to give it a second chance. He approached the thing slowly, with wide eyes and many a backward glance. But when Rob's repairs failed a second, then a third time, that was it for the tower. The thing had become an eyesore in the room. The cat pyramid went out on the curb, where some unknown animal lover picked it up. I only hope its new owner secured it with larger bolts than Rob managed to find. Or that he has a dumb cat.

Meanwhile, Rob's lap became Pretty Boy's late evening retreat. There he slumbered while Rob stroked his fur, and they enjoyed many a companionable few hours together. Until one evening, sitting in his leather chair with cat aboard, Rob was struck by an attack of gas. At which point—how do I put this delicately?—He did what any gentlemen tries not to do when anyone's around. Even a cat.

At the moment, Pretty Boy was nicely asleep. Beneath him, the chair suddenly rumbled, as though with an earthquake. From a state of utter relaxation, Pretty Boy sprang upwards to a height of more than three feet. As Rob watched in astonishment, the cat gyrated crazily as he rose, paws splayed out in four directions. He actually spun around like a gymnast with a complicated routine, performing moves Rob had never seen before, cat-wise or otherwise.

Rob said later, "I wondered how he gained so much traction—all this from a dead-asleep start." The cat did not remain airborne long. Once his feet returned to the land of trembling earth, he was off. He streaked across the family room and into the breakfast room, seeking, I suppose, some kind of flatulence-free oblivion.

Since then, Pretty Boy has tentatively returned to Rob's lap. But he now approaches his once-favored resting spot with the same hesitancy he once bestowed on the cat tower. So it behooves Rob to mind his manners. It would sadden him, and Tracy too, if he manages to permanently eject Pretty Boy from his lap.

We Left a Kid Once

According to our newspaper, the Prime Minister of England, David Cameron, recently left one of his kids in a pub. Knowing the Brits, half are laughing and the other half are writing indignant letters to their editors: "Cameron is an unfit father."

Call me what you like, but I've been guilty of the same crime. Or rather my husband, Rob, was at fault, because he was driving. As a family, we were on our way to Las Vegas. As we invariably did on those trips, Rob stopped in Baker to let us take a drink-and-potty break. That done, we merrily set off again. As usual, the noise inside our eight-passenger Buick was like the roar of a bullfight crowd—just before the goring.

Rob and I had six kids. I've always said that six was too many faces to keep on my mental screen at any one time. I'd often know someone was missing, but not always which one.

On this day we were twenty-five miles out of Baker when Bobby, our oldest, said, "Where's Eric?" Obviously Bobby's mental screen functioned better than mine.

"Eric?" I said. "Why he's right here, of course."

"No he isn't," said Bobby. "He's not in our row. Is he back there with you, Mom?"

I didn't have to look. "Oh, my God. I don't see Eric. Where is he?"

"Eric?" shouted Rob from the driver's seat. "Didn't he get in with the rest of us?" He was still speeding along.

"Don't think he made it," said our second son, Chris. "Count 'em, Mom. He's not here." Even back then, Chris (now a surgeon), never panicked.

"Stop, Rob! Stop!" I screamed. "We left Eric!"

"Good God!" said Rob, "I told everyone to get in." With his usual great reflexes, Rob spun the car around, right there in the middle of the highway. Within seconds he was speeding back in the other direction.

Finally our daughter spoke up. "I saw him going to the men's room. I never saw him come out."

"Eric was probably looking at his hair again," said Chris. "That's all he ever does. Probably still looking when we left."

"Hurry, Rob!" I yelled. "Hurry!" *Poor little boy, he's only ten.* "I can't believe we left him!"

For twenty miles I could hardly breathe … the longest twenty miles of my life. *Poor little boy*, I kept thinking. *The poor kid. What will he do?*

We arrived back at the gas station, nearly crazy with worry. Both Rob and I leaped out of the car and dashed into the little mini-mart, desperate in our haste.

There sat Eric on a stool, calmly licking a Popsicle. Strange as it seems, he didn't seem worried. He looked up at us and nodded. "The man told me you'd be back."

"Of course we'd be back," said Rob.

"Of course," I said. "You know we would." *God, I'm so glad to see you.* I stared at him hard, as though seeing him with new eyes.

And then, in my relief and gratitude I couldn't help thinking, *He really does have great hair.*

How to Kill Your Creativity

I just did it again—rushed into the family room with a great new idea.

I couldn't wait to tell my husband the core message for a new story—meaning something I meant to write immediately, starting in a few minutes. Unfortunately, I got the wrong response. He said "EEEYOOOGH!" exactly the way a teenager says it when you suggest he trim his father's ear hairs, or put on that new shirt from Aunt Helen ... or worse, stop showing his plumber's crack.

I don't know how to spell the sound, but you've all heard it. It's the world's briefest auditory conveyance of No Way, You've Got to be Kidding, or That's a Rotten Idea If I've Ever Heard One.

My idea for the new story fizzled like a party balloon with a pin prick. The creative air seeped out, faster and faster, and I just stood there, dismayed. And finally I said it. "Well, I've just broken the first rule of creativity."

Rob simply looked at me. He doesn't know the rule, and he wouldn't care about it if he knew. But he'll gladly give me his first reaction to anything he considers even slightly no good.

Have you caught on to the rule?

In case you haven't, the rule is, *Never share the first*

blush of a creative idea with ANYONE. Not until you've got it down on paper, not until the thing is mostly written and you can't easily un-write it.

If it was a dumb idea in the first place, you'll soon know. If it wasn't, you risk letting someone kill your tiny plant before it has a chance to take root.

Everyone who writes knows this rule, and no one better than I. My inner voice invariably says, *Don't share this,* and I should have listened, but I didn't; instead I rushed out to expose my great new vision to toxic fumes. Not too smart.

I finally said, "Nora Ephron's book is called, *I Remember Nothing.* Do you think that's a good title?" And he said No.

Well, that was some comfort, anyway. I'm sure Ephron has sold a million copies of this very funny book with the mediocre title. Except I happen to love it, bad title and all.

I'm also willing to bet she wrote the book first and asked for opinions last. Which means, among all her other talents, Ephron knew enough not to stifle her creativity.

IF YOU'RE THINKING GOOD THINGS, SAY THEM

IT'S SOMETHING I DO FROM TIME TO TIME.

If I'm out and about and happen to see a woman wearing an attractive hat, I might say offhandedly, "Cute hat!" Or similarly when an attractive shirt comes my way … "Love your top!"

I always get a look of surprise, then a smile. Of course it takes nerve to make personal comments to strangers—but who cares? The two of us invariably go our separate ways, and the only consequence is, we both feel a tad better about the world.

One evening we'd been to the Performing Arts Center, where Gustavo Dudamel led the Los Angeles Philharmonic in a stunning Bruchner symphony. Afterwards, we could have gone to the gala. Half the supporters were dressed for The Ritz and ready for a sumptuous, post-event dinner.

Then we learned the price: a thousand dollars. Each. Perhaps we didn't love the symphony quite that much. So instead, Rob and I went to *In and Out*. (My choice, as long as they continue serving juicy hamburgers, which for me compete with steak.)

Anyway, in the next booth sat three male high-schoolers and a younger boy, all wearing Loyola tee shirts. For awhile I watched them. They all had decent haircuts, their conversations were subdued, and their laughter not too raucous. I thought they were behaving extremely well. Good kids, the kind you wish there were more of.

When they got up to leave, I suddenly decided to run after them. Outside the restaurant I yelled to their retreating backs, "You kids seem like really nice people. I was impressed with how well you behaved." One of them turned around and grinned. They didn't actually stop, but I could tell that the one, anyway, was pleased.

As I re-entered the restaurant, a woman stood just inside. She said, "What did you tell those boys?"

I stared at her.

"I'm their mother. Just wondered what you said." Clearly, she was expecting the worst.

"It was a compliment," I said, and told her how impressed I'd been.

She smiled, and it was obvious I'd made her day. "People never say nice things to kids. It's always something negative. We just got back from a Loyola basketball game. They were pretty happy. I was hoping that wouldn't change."

"Well, I was thinking good thoughts," I said. "Why not say them?"

"Yes. Why not?" she said, and we shook hands.

She'd made my day, too. The whole episode took maybe five minutes. I can't vouch for the Loyola family, but for weeks those five minutes gave me little zings of pleasure.

Are You Ready to Publish?

Maybe. Maybe not. If you have doubts, you are probably not ready.

It's an impatient world out there—too many of us with too much to do. Too many newspapers to read, phone calls to make, e-mails to answer, meals to cook, minutes to spend exercising, dishes to wash.

Besides all that, you're writing a book. How much time do you give to your writing? One edit? Two? Possibly three?

How many people have read it? And what did they say?

"This is interesting." "I like it." "You've done a good job." "Nice piece." "An okay first chapter." "Keep going."

"Interesting" doesn't cut it. Nor do any of the other comments. These people are your friends, and they don't want to hurt your feelings. But their level of enthusiasm is tepid. And you know tepid when you see it on the page.

Your piece is clearly not good enough. None of these people are raving. So all you've done is make a decent first start. A dent. But the thing is not publishable. Not even close.

If you go "out there" with this work, even spend money to get it published, nobody will make the effort to read more than a few pages. (Except, maybe, your three best friends and your mother.) You will have spent time and energy on a piece of writing that needs lots more work.

Now wait!! Don't throw it away. Your idea is probably worth keeping. It's worth re-working. It's worth cutting, enriching, dissecting, made funnier. You are no dummy, you doubtless have unusual and interesting thoughts. Your work deserves to be read by others. Trust me on that one. Or rather, trust yourself. If you're reading this, you are not a throw-away writer.

The stark reality that few of us fully grasp is—good writing is a monumental task that takes hours of work. More work than any newbie ever imagines. It takes more refinement, more re-working, more polishing than most of us dreamed would be necessary. It takes more crafting than a Lamborghini.

But all that effort is a must. Unless you're willing to edit obsessively, your piece will never be ready for the larger world. Which means most people won't read it. So what's the point?

Okay, then, you've gone over your work a dozen times. It's finally begun to thrill you, to capture even your own over-exposed attention. You honestly believe it reads like the best stuff you've seen elsewhere. So you give it back to your friends.

Geronimo! Their critiques have changed. "This

is great!" "I love it!" "Powerful!" "I've given it to all my friends!" "Wonderful!" "Couldn't stop reading!" "I stayed up all night!"

These are the critiques that will finally send you to a publisher. And at last your baby stands a chance.

THE FOUR-MIRACLE FIRE

HE CALLED MY NAME IN A WAY I'D NEVER HEARD it before: "BABE! BABE!!" The voice was my husband's, and it penetrated right through the bedroom wall that separates us from the outside, rose above the whirring sounds of our bedroom air purifier, and drowned out the Santa Ana wind blowing outside—a real gale.

What I heard beyond the word itself was horror and urgency.

Oh my God! Oh my God! What is it?

Within seconds I was out of bed, tearing through the room and straight out the nearby door that leads to the backyard.

And there, beyond our bedroom wing, I saw him: Rob standing with a hose in his hand. And all around him … FIRE! Fire in the trees behind and above him, patches of fire among pine needles on the ground, sparks—in that terrible wind—flying above his head. To me, a virtual wall of fire with Rob standing in the middle.

"Rob! Stop it!" I screamed. "Rob! Run!"

Instead he stood there, hose moving, but his feet cemented in place. I screamed again, but he never acknowledged me—ignored me as if I wasn't there, or he couldn't hear my voice.

Getting nowhere, I raced back into the house and grabbed the nearest phone. It was dead. I ran to another, and strangely this one had a dial tone. Heart pounding hard enough to kill me, I did what only a half-crazed person might do: I dialed 411.

All I got, of course, was an automated voice asking for city and state.

Oh, God! Oh stupid. Stupid.

Ever more frantic, I re-dialed, this time 911. "Our house is on fire!" I cried to the responding woman, and with a partially restored brain managed to give her the correct street address. Next I called my daughter, once more saying without preamble, "The house is on fire!"

Just then our doorbell rang insistently. Once. Twice. Fists pounded on the front door. "Your house! It's burning!" cried the woman who stood there. Dimly I noticed she was a stranger, that she was thin and dressed all in black. "Get out! Get out now!" She leaned in to drag me out.

"I know! I know! My husband's in the backyard, and he won't leave."

"You get out, then!"

But I was in my nightie, and left her standing there while I rushed back to our dressing room for clothes. In seconds I was wearing the nearest shirt, the most grabbable pants. Shoes in hand, I ran back to the patio. With every fiber in my being I screamed at Rob to leave, but he ignored me. His hose turned one way, then another, while additional trees flamed and embers flew. And still he refused to budge.

Other neighbors came and literally pulled me outside. One of them went out back and tugged on Rob—a useless effort. Meanwhile, on the front walk I was bent over, trying to put on my shoes, trying to breathe. *Where are the fire trucks?*

"My husband!" I gasped. "He won't come!"

Our driveway was now full of neighbors, then a policeman ... then, finally, three huge fire trucks.

It was the firemen, about fifty of them the newspapers said, marching to the back in their thick yellow suits that finally made Rob surrender his hose.

For hours I was furious with my husband, couldn't stop being angry that he'd risked his life.

As a devoted group of us, neighbors and family, sat on a small retaining wall across the yard watching firemen douse the trees ... an adjacent woodpile ... a wooden fence ... our wooden patio cover ... and yes, the house, I could hardly speak to Rob. "Look at your shirt!" I cried, pointing to the charred holes across his shoulders.

"I shook a few embers out of my hair, too," he said.

He stood and paced restlessly, then told us, his small audience on the wall, how it all began:

"It was just before eight, and I was up, letting out the cat. Suddenly the cat stopped in the patio doorway and froze. All four paws were splayed, and he was staring toward the back. One long look and he streaked away. I wondered, What's he looking at? A squirrel?

"But his reaction was so extreme, I took a second look and saw what he'd seen: a pine tree in back, near the fence line, was totally on fire. The flames were headed down, lower and lower. Luckily, I had a hose on the patio, already turned on, and I rushed back there and began spraying."

Rob's efforts had clearly kept the flames from doing their worst.

Even as we watched the firemen, a sudden explosion of sparks sent them all jumping back. An electrical wire fell to the ground, and over by the bedroom wing, the live wire had to be cordoned off with yellow tape.

Suddenly Rob said, "Babe! Tell the firemen to stay off the roof! They'll break the shingles."

I ran around to the front. Too late. Five yellow suits were already up top, stomping around and throwing off concrete shingles.

The man from Edison who arrived later to retrieve the live wire told us what had happened: thanks to the fierce wind, a huge tree branch had fallen across the wires, knocked one against another, and produced enough sparks to ignite the pine tree. The wild wind did the rest.

Later that afternoon we recounted the miracles: Miracle One: That the fire did not start at two in the morning, with both of us asleep. We might not have known until the flames were right outside our bedroom. Or even inside.

Miracle Two: That Rob was up early—usually he isn't—and that the cat had flashed a warning.

Miracle Three: That Rob had a hose all ready and kept the house doused until the firemen got there.

Miracle Four: That our huge bedroom picture window and adjacent wing windows were all double paned. Directly confronted by flames from below and from a blazing woodpile six feet away, the outer panes shattered but the inner ones held. "If both panes had broken," a fireman said, "the wind would have blown the flames straight into the bedroom, and down through the house. I doubt we could have saved it."

As it was, for two days we had no water, no electricity, no gas, no Internet, no TV, no workable solar panels. Worst of all we had no phone, and my cellphone did not work anywhere near the house and never has. Which meant we couldn't call or be called by any of the dozen groups we needed to start restoring us to normal.

What we did have was a house in which every room in the bedroom wing reeked of smoke, making it too toxic to live in.

Thank God for our nearby daughter, Tracy, and husband Brad Hagen, who invited us to live in the "Hagen Hotel."

Happily, our insurance company, State Farm, reached from Tracy's house, responded immediately and with all the right people. They brought a contractor to drag away charred debris and a burned-up shed and fence, an interior crew who wiped down and cleaned every object in the bedroom area, including the walls, another bunch who took away all our hanging clothes to be cleaned, and yet another contractor who sealed off the bedroom area and set up an ozone machine which ran all night for two nights with the express purpose of killing odors.

A week later it was obvious that the rugs in that area needed to be replaced. The smoky smell had partially returned, meaning *something* was still giving off unlivable vapors.

It was Rob, though, who emerged as the original mixed blessing. For risking his life as he wielded the hose near our bedroom he was clearly an idiot. But for standing his ground and saving our home he was definitely a hero.

The *Real* Football Wasn't On Television

Never mind the Raiders and Cowboys. For the best football, come to Ladera Elementary School next Thanksgiving and see the game as it's supposed to be played. You might even get an email "e-vite" from a college athlete, as we did, or perhaps you'll simply hear about us on the street. For blocks in every direction, we're famous.

Around here football is actually a GAME. It's fun. Little kids get to "tackle" grownups, (okay, it's "tag" football), and they quickly learn to kick a football and even throw it—as long as they can successfully dodge the other twenty-three players (the numbers vary by the minute), and the two puppies loose on the field.

The grandparents, and that includes me, sit on the sidelines and watch. Right away I spotted a small blonde girl, about nine, who seemed to be a key member of every play. To my amazement, Taylor could zig-zag like a marine on an obstacle course. With the ball tucked against her pink and white striped shirt, she dodged, in quick succession, a UCLA volleyball player, an orthopedic surgeon, and a young man who'd just won a national

51

tennis tournament. Minutes later, Taylor made a clean, thirty-yard kick.

But that was peanuts compared to the sudden, surprising run by twelve-year-old Elizabeth who, on every day except Thanksgiving is a singer, not an athlete.

Along the periphery of the field, Lauren, eight, practiced her gymnastics with three back-flips in a row … while on the field behind her, brother Davis, ten but small for his age, caught the football just before it hit the ground. He didn't get far, though. The mother who is the country's number one fifty-and-over tennis player managed to grab his streamer.

Within a small circle, the game came to a momentary halt when the five-year-old lad from Denver threw an unexpected fit. One of the bigger boys simply picked him off the ground and set him down again outside the boundaries.

For a few seconds I tabulated the various ages. The surgeon, still a Sunday athlete, is sixty-one, the UCLA player is 23, his sister, a landscape architect, is 26. Still, the youngest player was five. I have no idea about the age or occupation of the man who arrived late, on his bicycle. All I gathered, really, is that his kids are whiz-bangs at sports and so eager to participate that they shortcut the journey by climbing over the school fence. Actually, so did several others. This is, after all, a neighborhood athletic field.

If you include a halftime water break, the game lasted an hour and a half. By the end I had no idea which team won—if indeed, scores were tabulated or anyone could tell who actually belonged to which squad. At times *they* knew, but I didn't. From afar there seemed to be a constant shifting of team loyalties as new participants arrived or others faded away, with large and small people reassigned to achieve some kind of balance.

Balance? Oh come on, there was no balance. Just a lot of sprinting, kicking, and throwing, with a few spectacular performances distributed up and down the age groups. And from us on the sidelines, a lot of wild cheering.

As they departed, everyone was sweaty and most were smiling. Good feelings prevailed. The smallest players dashed away without the need for extra praise. Hey, for awhile they'd been treated like adults. As far as I'm concerned, for the rest of Thanksgiving none of the professional games compared, even slightly, to this one.

Corruption Begins at Home

Here's the thing about my husband: he wants to save everything. In all our years of marriage, he's never met the item he doesn't want to keep (the only exception being rotten vegetables). A mantra rings in his head, which I know better than anyone because I hear it so often: "Keep that, Babe. We may need it some day."

Thus on his side of our kitchen we have a collection—dozens of used drink cups, both plastic and cardboard, complete in some cases with traces of dried cola. In our garage he stores old jelly jars, empty coffee cans, hunks of Styrofoam, strands of wire, dozens of once-filled vases, endless wicker baskets which once held flowers or gifts. Almost nothing is so mundane he sees the need to throw it away.

This is the man who once happened to follow a diaper truck onto a freeway offramp. The van took the corner too fast, and its back door flew open and a great white sack flew out onto the shoulder. The van never slowed, but Rob did. With his usual great reflexes, he brought his car to a fast halt near the fallen sack. *Rags!* He thought. *Dozens of perfect rags.!*

But when he picked up the sack a surprise was waiting. The diapers were dirty!

Any other man would have blown out his breath and dropped the sack like a hot coal. But not Rob. Knowing I'd kill him if he brought home that load, he went to the nearest Laundromat and ran the diapers through twice. Even today he chortles about how he gathered all those great rags.

Today was a kind of test, though. Now a few weeks past our Great Fire, this morning we had a crew of five men digging a trench—ready to replace our burned-up wooden fence with a block wall. About noon I looked outside to see men wheeling loads of dirt up a ramp and into a waiting truck. "Wow!" I cried, turning back to Rob, sitting in his usual chair. "You should see all the dirt they've hauled out of that trench!"

A mistake. "Dirt!" he cried, abruptly straightening. "They're hauling away our dirt?"

"Well, yeah. What else would they do with it?"

"But dirt is valuable," he said. "You pay good money for topsoil."

I couldn't believe what I was hearing. "This is a half acre, Rob. There's quite a lot of topsoil left."

"When they come to plant, the landscapers will need that dirt."

I just looked at him. Finally I said, "The landscapers will dig holes. They'll have their own dirt."

He finally subsided. He did not, as I feared, rush outside and order the diggers to leave our precious dirt in great humongous piles.

But dirt wasn't today's only issue. Outside near the pile of burned and discarded wooden fence was another pile—several dozen aluminum tubes that Rob brought home from our hang gliding company. In 1978. Over the years he's said, "Babe, somebody will need them some-day." Since they were mostly hidden by shrubbery, I never argued. But now all that shrubbery is gone. And there sit the tubes.

Today, as I looked at the two piles, fence scraps and tubes, I thought, *These tubes must go. We've had them long enough. Nobody will ever want them.* Unfortunately, I made the mistake of saying to Rob, "When they pick up the fence, they should take away the tubes."

He stared at me in horror. "Aluminum is worth money! They should be recycled!"

"How do you plan to do that?"

"I'll borrow a truck."

"A truck from whom? And who will load it? And how much do you think you'll get?"

"A lot. They're worth a hundred dollars, Babe. A hundred dollars, easy."

Inwardly I groaned. *Ten years from now those tubes will still be there.*

Suddenly I had an inspiration. I'll tell you what, Rob. If you let the contractor take away the tubes, I'll pay you fifty dollars."

His face softened, just a little.

Dear Lord, I'm onto something good. And then I thought, *Corruption begins at home.* "I'll make it a hundred dollars, Rob. Let the tubes go and I'll give you a hundred dollars."

With that, Rob broke into a big grin. "I'm selling out my principles for a hundred dollars. They should be recycled, you know."

"But think of the hassle. Let the contractor recycle them. If they're worth money, he'll do it. And you'll have the cash right now."

He didn't argue. He just smiled. But then, so did I. Never have I so looked forward to spending a hundred dollars. As we walked back into the house I thought, *I wonder how much it would cost me to clear out the garage?*

Getting Things Open

(The following is a chapter from my book, *SO YOU'RE SEVENTY ... SO WHAT? How to Love the Years You Thought You'd Hate*. However, the laments in this chapter lap over into other age groups—in fact, they apply to everyone).

The Other Day I had a nasty fight with a bag of peanuts. I was sitting on a plane and starving—with a little bag of nuts that was as defiant as one of my cats, the one that won't let you pet him in the morning. Here was a bag that wouldn't let you break it open—not from the left, the right, nor across the top.

Rob says the core issue was arthritis and I swear it wasn't. It was idiot manufacturing. I'm no weaker than I was a few years ago, and no dumber, either, so surely I can always outwit a mere cellophane bag. *There must be a tiny slit*, I thought, examining the bag from all sides, *or an arrow, or an indentation that tells me where to pull.*

Doesn't every manufacturer offer a clue about retrieving his product? Even if, like my favorite brand of bacon, the clue doesn't work?

Apparently not. There I sat with a clueless bag ... and a growing sense that, ounce for ounce, there is no stronger material in everyday use than this peanut wrap. They ought to use it for parachutes.

Finally, with both hands pulling in opposite directions, I tried separating front from back, but the two sides clung to each other like desperate lovers.

Never mind that I consider myself reasonably strong and my fingernails even stronger, the bag won out. Unless I was willing to chew up the package in one lump, cellophane and all, I was doomed to go peanutless.

I looked around for something ... a sharp edge on the seat, a protruding nail, but all I saw with tool potential was the guy sitting across the aisle.

With a smile I leaned across and handed him my little bag. "Please, can you open this?"

He was obviously still in his prime—loaded with testosterone. With a mighty wrench he pulled on the bag, letting only a peanut or two escape before he handed it back, nodding in some kind of personal triumph.

"Thanks," I said. But I was thinking, *Oh, how godly are men. Men who can open things.*

ANY THINKING PERSON CAN SEE THERE'S A CONspiracy afoot in our country—a conspiracy to make us eat less by making each and every ingredient difficult or impossible to get at.

When Rob and I go to a ball game and order a hot dog, I sometimes forget that the mustard comes in flat packets of a few drops each, so you need seven of them ... that it takes vampire teeth to make the first puncture, then a mighty twist from what are soon mustard-covered fingers. Then a napkin to remove the portion that squirted onto your shirt. Such is the level of unpleasantness that sometimes, before I order the hot dog, I check out the mustard. If it doesn't flow freely, I skip the dog and go for the ice cream.

The trend toward packaging in open-proof containers is now everywhere. And never mind that I do have arthritis. The last time I bought a curling iron it was sealed up with stiff plastic on the front and impenetrable cardboard on the back—the kind against which even the strongest, non-arthritic hand is useless.

Which goes as well for Rob's new screwdriver ... enclosed in a container that required a much larger screwdriver to stab it open—except he ended up using a screwdriver plus a hammer.

You soon realize this problem isn't *us*—it's *them*!

While I was speaking at a conference recently, a woman graciously handed me a bottle of water. But it was one of those newer bottles, with the cap so ultra narrow it provided no place to grip. I had to put it aside and go on talking. As a friend said later, "To drink the water you have to behead the bottle."

The tightly-screwed jelly jar lid is no longer symbolic of all that is wrong with today's industrial packaging.

Rob, no longer a kid (and in spite of sore fingers), can open the toughest jelly jar with a fierce grimace and a loud grunt. But give him a little squishy container of mustard, or worse, a wrench that is contained within one of those see-through packages—where you can view the tool but never quite reach it—and he's as frustrated as though he was once again a boy of ten.

"It's sealed for the ages," he says, pounding the container with a butcher knife.

Never a patient man, he finally tosses the thing on the carpet. "No sense my trying to open it. They designed this package for the Time Capsule. To break into it you'd need the Jaws of Life."

Few of these problems have much to do with our being Seventy. It's only because of living this long that we've personally witnessed the evolution of wrapping things up—from the simple dropping of merchandise off the shelf into an open brown paper bag, to the demonic packaging of today.

One of my friends noted that you can purchase a special kind of scissors for opening such containers. Which I'd buy, if only they were loose on the shelf. But they're not, they're sealed up like priceless museum pieces. Even my cat, who can dismember the toughest rat, would not be able to reach it.

For you women who don't carry scissors in your purse, you can just forget about the peanuts.

A World Turning Upside Down

As an author, I don't know which side is up.

For all of you, like me, who see your everyday lives morphing faster than you ever dreamed possible, let me add that nothing is changing quicker, or with more uncertainty, than book publishing. Those of us on the inside can only wonder and shake our heads. As authors we try to adjust, but few of us can predict which of our books will sell best—if at all—or in what format. Will old-fashioned paper even be involved?

Only a handful of years ago, nobody thought book stores might soon become obsolete. Yet while a few still stand their ground in certain malls, looking formal and important, the "Grande Look" is only a façade, like a necktie on a derelict. Inside, most book stores resemble college libraries. At every table, students with coffee cups and laptops earnestly study and type. Meanwhile those few adults who find their way inside are invariably in a hurry, searching for a particular book. Since clerks no longer recommend titles to their favorite customers, adults no longer browse.

Part of this is the fault of the chain bookstores themselves. In their eagerness to rid themselves of competing independents, they also killed off the eager, pseudo-librarian clerks, who once "sold" their readers the world's best literature. Today, the chain stores are not known for selling anything; all they do is display. Which Costco—or your best friends—do just as well.

Meanwhile, we authors are scrambling to become known in that mysterious and semi-visible world of the Net. Those of us who aren't kids any longer eventually discover we need expertise to help us—wizards on steroids—so I'm finding computer mavens to make me and my books Internet-visible. Will this help me sell some of the volumes in my garage?

I honestly don't know.

As part of this year's vow to constantly update my website, I have put there the first chapter of my recently re-published memoir, *Higher Than Eagles*.

There, then, is the story of our hang gliding years with our oldest son, Bobby, who fought his father and fought his asthma, but "found" himself in the sport of hang gliding. Sports Illustrated wrote of him: "Like Paul Elvestrom, the great Danish sailor, he seems now to own a special part of the wind that not even he can see and no one else can find."

If you end up reading this chapter—and liking it— you can e-mail me and I'll ship you an autographed copy. Or you can get an e-book copy from Amazon. Or, good heavens, you can go to a book store. With luck, they'll order a copy.

How Did I Get in the Twilight Zone?

AND HOW DID THIS STORY MAGICALLY DISAPPEAR from Chapter Thirteen?

For a month I've had a watch problem. It all began when my reliable solar wrist watch stopped abruptly, and nothing short of mouth-to-mouth could revive it. Now, after some dozen jeweler visits with other watches that gulp down a new battery, politely submit to a cleaning, then fail to run longer than a day-and-a-half, the "watch thing" is playing games with my head.

Several days ago, in the midst of all this, my computer also failed. Like other non-techies, I have a love-hate relationship with that piece of technology. When it works I adore it. When the thing fails, I'm ready to do what a few men have done to their televisions—take a pistol and shoot out its heart.

That morning my e-mail messages refused to "come out" or "come down" or "show up"—whatever it is they do. Even tapping the send/receive button over and over like the Morse Code produced nothing. Since the machine was working just fine the night before, I gave it a few hours to rest.

Finally, in desperation, I began calling people who weren't answering. The wonderful man who set up my web site. My web server. My doctor son. I was ready to call Steve Jobs. Except I ran out of time.

Best to leave the balky thing alone and hope, like a mule, the animal might yet come around.

That night, at 9:30, in desperation I called Cox. To my amazement, an actual person answered the phone. Graciously, he put me through enough routines to re-start the *Queen Mary*, but his efforts produced nothing useful on my screen.

At last he said, "You know, we don't actually support Microsoft Outlook." By then he'd given me a new email password, and a few keys to a secret kingdom of Cox emails that I never knew existed. Not a great site, but okay as a fall-back for the truly desperate. "Guess you'll have to call Microsoft."

"But Microsoft charges," I whined. "For every min-ute. They cost a bundle." Over the phone came a quiet sigh. "Best I can do."

We signed off and I looked down at my newly-re-paired watch. It was still 9:30. I stared at the face, at the non-moving second hand. Suddenly I realized it had been 9:30 for quite a few hours.

A creepy feeling came over me and I began thinking *Twilight Zone*. The computer was down. My just-fixed watch was down. Was I dead and didn't know it?

Could I even walk away from here? Taking a deep breath, I pinched my leg and was relieved to feel the pain. Still … my computer stopped. My watch stopped. Would my heart stop, too?

I was actually afraid to go to bed. *Gotta stay awake and keep breathing.*

Downstairs, Rob heard the story over and over, until he finally said, "I've heard it three times, Babe. That's enough. Let's go to bed. It's one in the morning."

I was thinking, "How do we know it's one? My watch has been ticking perfectly for three days. It says 9:30."

I opened my mouth, but he gave me THE LOOK.

Next day, instead of paying a ransom to Microsoft, I called Cox again—for a lady tech's long and useless session, until finally she said as an afterthought, "You might try turning the computer off and back on."

I did. And the miracle-on-my-desk actually worked.

Back at the jewelers, the man took out the latest battery and found it dead. We talked *Twilight Zone*. As he installed yet another battery, he said, "This really does smack of voodoo."

And indeed it does. Because this morning that watch is once again staring at me with its tongue lolling. Nothing is moving. The silence is ominous. Voodoo is circling my wrist. For three hours, now, my watch has read 8:00 a.m.

Revenge of the Jilted Draperies

IT HAPPENED RECENTLY AT A WRITER'S CONFERENCE.

Just as I was finishing a lecture and starting a drawing to give away books, a participant stood up unexpectedly and began describing her reactions to the last chapter in my memoir, *A Circus Without Elephants*. She said, and I blushed, "It's one of the funniest scenes I've ever read." And she went on from there.

I didn't how to respond. Finally I just said, "Can I take you everywhere?"

Here, after a short preamble, is the scene she was talking about:

Renovating the House

NOBODY COULD UNDERSTAND WHY WE WERE ADDING on to the house. "Your children are pretty much grown," a friend pointed out reasonably enough. "Why do you need more space?"

Rob answered with a grin, "We always add a room

whenever a kid leaves. Makes perfect sense to us. When all the kids are gone, we'll build a castle."

I nodded. "Well actually, I got tired of eating breakfast on top of yesterday's mail. I know it's ridiculous—spending all this money for a place to put the mail. But we don't pretend to be rational."

The question of whose idea it was to expand the whole rear of the house and add a breakfast room shifted from week to week. In Rob's mind "our idea" became "her idea" as the kitchen began to resemble a hobo's digs, with appliances missing everywhere, like a mouth with half its teeth, and exposed water pipes staring at us from the sub flooring, and the walls sporting nail holes but no cabinets.

It continued to be "her idea" in January, as I hauled buckets of dirty dishes to the bathtub and the temperature in the open part of the house dropped below forty and a raccoon came in, and I do mean IN. There he was one night in the family room, standing his ground defiantly, eying us through his mask.

It became "our" project once more as the kitchen and family room began to look sleek and modern, twice as nice as before.

"This has been an unbearable year," Rob declared, and vowed he would absolutely never do anything major to the house again, come hell or high water . . .. and high water was what we seemed in danger of getting, because the toilets in two mostly unused bathrooms had developed small leaks, and water began seeping onto the floors when we weren't looking, and the bathroom floors were slowly rotting into mush. I expected to go back there one day and step right through the sub floor onto the dirt.

And sure enough, it wasn't long before we had to tear up the bathrooms, too.

The house renovations began to consume all aspects of our lives. Eventually the two of us acquired a cavalier spirit, a "What the hell" attitude, which spread like recklessly sown seeds over the entire house ... and meant we bought things we didn't necessarily need, like new living room drapes.

The old drapes might never have become part of the family history had Rob's car not failed about then, forcing him to borrow our son's disreputable Cutlass.

When he went out to commandeer Kirk's car for an errand, Rob found the driver's seat literally agape at the seams. He searched for something to throw over it—the closest thing at hand being one of the discarded draperies. Rob tossed the drape over the seat, letting the hooks dangle free in back. Since the car was, as usual, out of fuel, he headed for the nearest gas station.

He couldn't have known that the drapes figured out they'd been rejected, that they'd developed an attitude, made worse by the fact he was now sitting on them.

As Rob drove, he felt the drape slipping, working

its way down the seat. When at last he got out of the car to pump gas he knew at once he wasn't alone; the drape had come with him.

It took only seconds to grasp the situation: the hooks had managed to embed themselves in the back of his bulky-knit Scottish sweater, and now here he was, standing in the gas station with a ten-foot-long, open-weave, gold-threaded cape flowing from his shoulders … and not only that, it was pleated!

Rob realized immediately he had a serious personal appearance problem. He glanced around, all-too-aware that he bore a remarkable similarity to King Henry the Eighth. Reaching around to disentangle himself, he quickly found that the hooks had dug in with fiendish cunning, just at that point in his back where he couldn't reach. He twirled and squirmed and shimmied, but all his efforts to free himself merely drew unwelcome attention to his bizarre predicament.

As he spun around in his dangling cape, other customers began reacting with startled double-takes, then fast aversions of the eyes. The man fueling the nearest car stood at an odd angle, trying to keep one eye on the gas nozzle and the other on Rob. Rob knew all too well what the man was thinking. *I've gotta get away from this nut case.*

There are times when Rob's sense of humor utterly fails him, and this was one of them. Ever more exasperated, he clawed at his shoulders like a demented Shakespearian monarch. But the more frantic he became, the more the hooks behaved like porcupine quills, tightening their grip, until it appeared Rob might be wearing the living-room drapes for the rest of the day.

By now a few customers were quietly leaving the gas station, some without filling their tanks, and Rob was truly desperate. He considered disrobing right there among the gas pumps, pulling sweater and drape up over his head and ridding himself of both.

But the sweater was tight and hard to remove under normal conditions, and the drape was so long it dragged the sweater down in back—and he couldn't begin to shed the two without scissors ... or a chain saw. Besides, he didn't like the idea of adding a strip tease to the rest of his already-under-appreciated performance.

Feeling anything but regal, he kept his head down and filled his tank. Finished, he gathered his remaining dignity, strode purposefully across the station, paid the bill to a clerk who refused to look him in the eye, and sauntered back, trailing his cape as if it were his normal attire. "One of the longest walks of my life," he said.

Once at home, he walked into the house muttering, "Here, Babe, get me out of this damn thing!"

I took one look at his drifting, open-weave raiment and burst out laughing. With the drapes dragging behind him, my husband did not look like the king of anything. He was Carol Burnett without the curtain rod. I was laughing so hard it was difficult to make my fingers do what they had to do. "How did you happen to acquire this lovely garment?" I asked.

"Well, it certainly wasn't deliberate!" As he began to explain, I thought I was going to split something—I was so doubled up, practically hysterical.

The next time I saw the draperies they were heaped in a trash barrel near the curb, which, considering who put them there, was an act of wanton recklessness. For the man who never throws away anything, trashing those drapes indicated profound disgust, and meant Rob never, ever, wanted to see them again.

A New Loss of Innocence

It started with the atomic bomb. I was just a child when I learned that our U.S. scientists had figured out how, with one finger on one button (or maybe several buttons) to drop a bomb out of an airplane and incinerate half a country.

The knowledge provoked a twist in my psyche. For years I had childish nightmares, woke up sweating because I'd dreamed that the world around me was exploding in a mass of flame.

Ever since, I've argued with everyone, including my husband, that this was the worst sin any country could commit—developing, then using, a weapon that had the potential of destroying an entire country. "But it saved endless American lives," Rob said, "maybe even mine. All the men who would have died invading Japan."

Nevertheless.

This week it happened again. Suddenly my computer screen came alive with horrifying news. "A Malaysian passenger jet has been shot down over Ukraine."

My first thought: *What was a passenger plane doing, flying that low?*

The awfulness arrived in stages. Within an hour we learned it wasn't THAT LOW. The plane was flying at

33,000 feet! Then another brutal fact: 298 souls on board. (An NTSB term).

The final stage arrived several days later, via the *Los Angeles Times.* We learned that such a missile, developed by Russia, can reach a target at 70,000 feet! Higher than any passenger jet ever flies.

Is this terrible news common knowledge? I wondered. "Did you know that such a weapon existed?" I asked Rob, who reads everything, and all the time.

"No," he said. "I only knew about shoulder launchers that could catch a plane on takeoff or landing. I've worried about them—how easy it would be."

"You know what this means," I said, and all my warm feelings about the NTSB and TSA and how they constantly protect airplanes began frosting up. "No plane, anywhere, is safe from its enemies."

"That's about right," he said. And neither of us mentioned our airline tickets, already purchased, for flights over Europe. When you lose your innocence it's a hard condition to retrieve—or even talk about.

Suddenly Pandora's Box is once again wide open. (For just a second, there, I felt like dropping an atomic bomb on Russia.)

Bad Beginnings Kill Books

Unless you're Tom Clancy, your book can't survive a lukewarm start.

And hey, even Clancy messed up ... in one of his books he devoted an entire first chapter to a description of the White House. My attention drifted until by the seventh page I finally stopped reading. It's possible the story eventually recovered, but I'll never know.

How writers craft their first lines, their first paragraphs, their first page, is everything. Bad beginnings aren't just bad—they're fatal. New writers seldom "get it," haven't an inkling how to create a gripping first page ... though a great many think they do. What they don't realize is, with a weak start, nobody will read the rest. It's worth spending hours, days, to make sure your beginning is extraordinary.

Recently I was a speaker at a Wyoming writers conference, where I critiqued seven Advance Submissions, whose qualities ranged from poor to nearly professional.

Yet one thing all had in common: nobody knew where to start.

I still remember some of those slow first pages: a young woman taking cookies to her aging grandmother; another girl traveling to Florida on a train, idly musing about her changing life; a couple setting up a tent on the beach; a young girl driving into a strange town, reasons unknown.

Nothing happening anywhere.

Compare those beginnings to this from an author I recently interviewed: In Las Vegas a young woman falls out of a tour helicopter and lands in the middle of the pirate show on Treasure Island.

Now THAT'S a beginning.

Not all beginnings need be this extreme. But the book must open in the middle of something dramatic. A beginning can be compared to someone falling into a rushing river … and any minute he'll plunge over the waterfall.

Beginnings start at a moment of crisis, after which the characters' lives change forever, and nothing will ever again be the same.

When I speak to memoir writers I ask, "What's the most dramatic thing that ever happened to you?" And when they explain, I say, "Start there. Then backtrack and tell us how you got there and why this terrible, or amazing thing happened."

Think of the book, *Into Thin Air* in which a mountain climber attempts to reach the top of Mount Everest. Guess where the book starts … at the top of Everest. So you know the hero reached his goal—but still, fascinating story questions remain. How did he get there? What happened along the way? What about the people who never achieved their dreams—who instead may have died?

If you need examples of great starts to novels, you might look at my book, *Damn the Rejections, Full Speed Ahead*, and read the chapter on Beginnings. I've got some great ones.

Meanwhile, in your own work, as you begin Chapter One, think DRAMA. CATASTROPHE. EXCITEMENT. PERIL. Anything less won't do.

Motherhood Isn't for Sissies

My son is an alcoholic—with all the horror that implies. At times, in the past, he used drugs, too—even the kind that make you not quite human, or as they once said about the scary people, he was "mad."

Like other mothers of abusers, I've had every emotion about him that it's possible to have—sadness for the years he's spent in prison, anger that he seems unable, or even unwilling, to do anything about his problem, fury during those times that he's attacked me—never physically, though at times it felt physical. When someone curses you at the top of his lungs it's like a physical attack.

Sometimes I've wished him out of my life forever. Or alternatively, I've wished him back in prison. At the worst times … well, no mother should even think it.

But then came a few good times. The moments when the sober Kirk helped me clean up our yard after a fire. The times he helped around the kitchen, or took out the trash, or just "swept up" without being asked. All those too-few moments when he's shown that under the alcoholic layers there's a good human being.

Today he was at our house making calls, trying to find yet another sober-living house that was willing or able to take him. Looking for another "start" to his very sad life. Though Rob and I have vowed he will never live here again, today I relented. He'd been calm today. And good. And philosophical. I said, "Okay, Kirk, go ahead and spend the night in your old room. For tonight we'll skip putting you in a motel. Just sleep here."

Suddenly I realized he was no longer in the family room with us. Instead, I found him in his old bedroom, sleeping soundly. At peace for once. Home again once more. My old mother-feelings welled up as I stood looking down at him. After all the tortured nights he's been in terrible places, how right it seemed that our son was once again sleeping serenely in his own bed.

This peace, this "rightness" can't last, and I know it. For now, I'm experiencing the return of mother love. The love that surrounded him when he was born and lasted a great many years. I realized, standing there, that it was possible to feel once more as I once felt about him. Unequivocal love.

I don't understand this mechanism—how it's possible to have so many different feelings about one human being. I called another son, Chris, trying to explain. He said, "If you're having a good interval, Mom, enjoy it. Hang on to it and cherish it. We all know, there haven't been many such moments."

I guess what I'm trying to say is, motherhood is complicated. And even more, so is love.

Kids Talk Funny

I DIDN'T EXPECT A NOTE LIKE THAT—EVEN FROM an adult granddaughter who's good with words. Her handwritten card started with: "Happy Birthday," and after a few thoughts about my apparent youthfulness, ended with, "We love you to the moon and back."

This from a grown woman, who's now married. But for me she sets a new standard in declarations of love.

As an author, perhaps even more as a parent, I've cherished my kids' words as much as their pictures … possibly because I've carried some of their best quips in my head, ready to share at the drop of an appropriate moment.

Saving words began with my youngest brother, who at age six, stood in our front hall with his trousers gone and his young legs an awful display of shredded skin and dripping fluids. "Oh, Hilary," I cried, "What happened?" I was sixteen.

"My legs are burned," he said. And then he looked at me with understanding beyond his years. "I'm pretty badly hurt for a little boy, aren't I?"

I was too shocked to answer—that he'd so perfectly grasped the situation … also that he'd managed to couch it in such perfect English. Though terribly scarred, he survived. Yet it was his prescient and awful statement at age six I could never forget.

Later came my own kids: Chris, barely walking, who took my hand as we went trick-or-treating. At the first house, a lady handed him a wrapped hard candy. He stood for a second staring at the yellow treat. Then he reached out, handed it back, and said, "O-pen."

From babyhood, my kids knew I had a thing about choking. So when our oldest, Bobby, went with me to the park, he noticed a big, friendly dog with a tennis ball in its mouth. Leaning into the dog's face, Bobby reached for the ball and said earnestly, "You might choke yourself, honey."

I wish back then somebody had given me the advice I give my kids and grandkids. When it comes to your children, don't just take pictures. Write down what they say. You'll soon cherish their words as much as their images.

So there's our grandson, Dane who, at about four, watched Rob's ninety-year-old mother, Ruth, lean on her cane as she hobbled out our front door. After she was well gone, Dane leaned over an imaginary stick and slowly tottered across the family room. "I can do the old thing," he said.

Only a year later, Ruth died. On hearing this, Dane asked innocently, "Is she dead as a doornail?"

On a daily basis, I'm reminded that my grandkids

feel free to make up their own family labels. One of the boys calls me "Babe." Another addresses me as "Grandmama." And then there's the one who occasionally whispers close to my ear, "Graham crackers."

Now, with the next generation, I've been writing down what the young ones are saying. One day my little relative, Nora, then threeish, went to Irvine Park with her older brother, Oliver, five. All the way out there, Oliver regaled the adults by reciting capitols of states. Once at the park, without telling anyone, Nora rushed off to find a bathroom. The adult who caught up with her scolded her gently about dashing off without adult supervision. Nora took it only so long. Finally she broke in and turned to her brother. "Oliver, talk to her about the states."

As if I didn't know it before, I realize our grandkids' written words are just as precious as things they've said. And I have it here on paper, expressed better than any words of mine. For the first time, someone loves me to the moon and back.

A Public Senior Moment

Rob happened to be standing at the counter of Der Weiner, ordering his usual Polish, when somebody tapped him on the shoulder. He turned and saw that the person was a lady, quite tiny and aged … and also that she was Japanese. To his surprise, she asked, "What year were you born?"

Before he could answer, she said, "I was born in 1926. What year were you born?"

"A year later than that," said Rob. "Why?"

Ultimately, as usually happens with Rob, the two exchanged stories—not only that she was from the Big Island in Hawaii—and somehow didn't speak Japanese—but, to her surprise, that he and his family had recently been there.

Before I go further, let it be known that Rob is smarter than I am, smarter than lots of people, and always "with it." He regularly astounds me as we watch *Jeopardy*. Some evenings he gets more right answers than the contestants. "How did you know the name of that river … the one that runs between Laos and Thailand?" I ask.

"I don't know how I know. Must have heard it somewhere."

"And you knew what year the *Hindenburg* caught

fire. How did you happen to get that?"

"I saw it in the paper," he said. "I remember the exact year and month—and how old I was at the time." He looked at me. "It's one of those events I'll never forget."

"Well," I said, "I remember reading about the *Hindenburg,* too. Besides the awfulness of the description, and grasping that the blimp's gondola was full of people and the whole thing came down in flames, all other facts escape me."

"I felt like I was there," he said.

All the above is a preamble to the fact that Rob always has his wits about him, that without half trying he remembers details most of us forget, that in spite of being a senior citizen, he's able to retrieve information from some unseen encyclopedia of little known facts. He gives no appearance of "losing it."

But back to the tiny Japanese lady and how it all began. After they'd exchanged birthdates he of course asked, "Why?"

And that was when she tentatively touched a spot near his waist. "I was just curious," she said. "See this tag?"

Rob looked down and suddenly grasped her assumption—that he was an elderly man living alone, that he needed somebody to put him straight.

She withdrew her hand and gave him a kindly look. "Your shirt is inside out."

Fixation on my Mailbox

For years I've had this thing about my mailbox; it was kind of like an affair.

Unable to stay away, I ran out to gaze hungrily into its face two or three times a day, this container that seemed to vibrate as I approached, thrilled by the knowledge that it held my future tight in its metallic grasp.

Would my short story come flinging back, or would I get a letter saying I'd sold it? Would an editor write, asking to see the rest of my book? Or would I find its opposite … my own ten chapters, whole and untouched by human eyes, with a few cold sentences attached? Would I leave my lover on winged shoes, or would I slouch away, dragging myself back to the house in a haze of rejection?

At times I knew my fixation on the mailbox bordered on kinky.

But hey, e-mail has made unsavory fixations like mine a whole lot worse. These days it's my computer screen I rush to embrace with my eyes, like a clandestine lover. I run upstairs first thing in the morning, several times midday, and in the last moments before bed. Will my screen yield what I want so desperately … an agent? Or even better, a publisher?

If you think I'm crazy, let me tell you about my friend whose book is agented, and now sent out to eight publishers. She goes to the grocery store with her cell phone clutched in her fingers. "I can hardly pick up more than one tomato at a time," she says, "or even an avocado, because I have this thing in my hand. Every few minutes I need to peek at my screen and see if anything came in. Like one tomato ago."

She finally admitted that a mere few weeks earlier, her phone suffered a brief, e-mail-free breakdown. "It was a relief," she said, "to have both hands usable. I could go to the grocery store and get my stuff in half the time. Of course during that week I was always rushing home again, tearing up the stairs to visit my computer." She sighed. "You don't know what it's like to be emotionally tied like this—to a laptop Lothario."

"Oh, but I do," I said. "Between me and my virtual lover, there's this flight of stairs. I don't gallop anywhere else, but I'm a lickety-split, stairs-to-the-computer climber. As soon as I sit down, I become a dewey-eyed screen gazer, pouring my very soul onto this blue field with the white letters, staring at it with all the hope, all the eagerness I once bestowed on my teenage boy friends. Or on my mailbox."

Oh, Lord, I thought, *my husband won't like this.* Or worse, he'll think I'm crazy.

After this frank admission to the world I can see a

problem arising in a somewhat larger arena. *Everyone will think I'm nuts.*

Disappointment Isn't Defeat

I shouldn't have checked my e-mail. Labor Day night, after a warm and often hilarious family dinner, I should have stayed away from my upstairs office; I should have kept hope alive for another day.

But no, I had to go look.

And there it was—what felt like a fatal blow—a final rejection for my latest book, *The Tail on my Mother's Kite*. After all these years I'm used to rejection and seldom grieve longer than a few minutes. But this refusal hit me hard, like a timber falling on my head. And all because of how it began.

After reading the first ten emailed chapters, an editor had written back, "We've enjoyed your manuscript so far, and we'd love to read the rest of it … We look forward to hearing from you and reading your wonderful manuscript."

Of course I was thrilled and sent it off immediately.

Even with those magic words ringing in my head, I tried not to hope too much. For a month I mentioned it to friends only vaguely, kept my expectations low. In this business, soaring hope must be tempered with diminished expectations, or your psyche would shrivel under the onslaught. You'd give up. Tear up your work.

Go jump off a bridge.

Actually, I could have given up years ago. Sometimes, during the 14 years it took to polish and re-polish and finally sell *Higher Than Eagles* I thought, *What's the use? Why am I still trying?* The book gathered hundreds of rejections ... I never counted them all, there were too many. Yet after it was published it attracted awards—and five movie options, including from Disney and the producers of *Northern Exposure.* Recently a fan told me, "I never read a book twice, but now I'm reading *Higher Than Eagles* for the second time."

For a few days after Labor Day I had this big lump in my stomach, so intrusive I didn't feel like eating—but hey, I lost three pounds! I fought back the impulse to go wailing to family and friends. *They all have their own problems.*

Never a moaner himself, Rob jumped in to find a new name for the book so I could re-pitch agents who'd already rejected me. Yesterday he suddenly sat up in bed and proclaimed, "I've got the new title, Babe! *"Heiress on the Prowl."*

He was serious.

Thanks to Rob and something in me that doesn't give up, I'm back working again, trying to figure out what killed the second half of my book ... trying to devise a new title that um ... rises above prowling heiresses. For no good reason my optimism is back.

It must help that I'm half German, and you know how Germans are—you can corner them and threaten them and show them no mercy, but they never quit. I guess most of you don't know this, since I've long been disguised as a Wills ... but my maiden name is Klumpp.

Danger From the Sea

When they moved into their condo, the young newlyweds were perfectly healthy. Our granddaughter, Jamie, and husband, Mike, were lucky enough to have a tennis court mere yards away. Both athletes, they took frequent advantage of the lighted courts and played singles after work and doubles with friends on weekends.

But then something began going wrong. Both Mike and Jamie started having allergy-like symptoms: stuffy noses, sneezing, itchy eyes and trouble sleeping. In spite of a regular bedtime routine—in bed by 10:30, up at 7:30—every day they woke up exhausted.

Mike's symptoms grew worse. His ears began dripping liquid, staining their new pillows. His eyes were so dry and itchy he began to suffer migraines. After one severe bout with migraine that included tingling in his face, he ended up in the emergency room. Yet the doctors could find nothing wrong.

"This isn't normal," said Tracy, our daughter, and she suggested the two get a new mattress, which they did. Nothing changed. Then the couple discovered mold in their bathroom, and at great expense had the shower removed and replaced. But still their symptoms persisted.

If anything, both of them were worse.

One day a desperate Mike, with a degree in microbiology, stalked into their bathroom and said, "Maybe this sea fan has something to do with it." The purple sea fan sat on a specially-designed stand right next to the shower. It was so beautiful Jamie had decorated the bathroom around it. Her towels were purple and the walls were painted a lighter hue. Everyone agreed—the bathroom was lovely.

With her own degree as a landscape architect, Jamie said immediately, "Mike, the sea fan is dead. That can't possibly be a problem." The issue was shaping up as a battle between college degrees. She added, "But if you'd like to do an experiment, that's okay with me." So Mike moved the plant to the garage.

Four days later, for the first time, Jamie and Mike got a good night's sleep; they woke up with cleared sinuses and new energy.

Jamie immediately Googled the Gorgonia Sea Fan and the truth came out; the purple variety was prone to acquiring a fungus, Aspergillus. The high incidence of Aspergillus on sea fans was linked to a 17 percent increase of asthma in Caribbean children. For anyone with a compromised immune system, Aspergillus could be a deadly fungus.

Now, with their own ornament positioned so that warm shower vapors washed over it constantly, sending toxins into their adjoining bedroom, the pair were slowly being poisoned. Mike's sister, a doctor, declared, "The reason you kids survived as well as you did is that you were both basically healthy. That sea fan could have killed someone in poor health."

When I suggested to Jamie that she ought to stuff it so deep in the trash that nobody could resurrect it, she said, "One of our quick-witted friends said, "Don't throw it away. Don't you have an enemy?" Then she laughed. "And to think I rescued that thing off a beach in the Caribbean. We'd gone to a deserted island in Virgin Gorda, and the fan had washed up on shore." She threw me a look. "How was I to know?"

She added, "After we learned the truth, Mike was so annoyed that for several days he was anything but loving. Finally he brought up our long-ago Caribbean trip. In a crabby voice I hear only rarely, he said, 'I told you not to bring home that damn Sea Fan.'"

MINING FOR MIRACLES

A COUPLE OF WEEKS AGO, ONE OF MY BLOG READERS remarked—in response to my piece about disappointment —"It isn't over 'til you quit." A simple idea and of course not original, yet with profound implications. Think about it:

That must have been the attitude of Olympic runner Louis Zamperini during his agonizing hours (weeks), of survival on a raft at sea. And later when he was tortured endlessly by the Japanese. Because of the account in "Unbroken" we know Zamperini made it back to the United States—only to face a new enemy: alcoholism. Yet he lived to be 97 … and when he was well into his nineties, he still gave speeches, and I know this, because one of my friends heard him.

Examples of not giving up keep coming to me. Not long ago I spent hours (in Boston) talking to my 55-year-old nephew, Jim Klumpp, who had just returned from a hike of 2,200 miles. For nearly five months he walked over 20 miles a day, the entire length of the Appalachian Trail. He wore out six pairs of shoes and could only take in enough calories by eating two Snicker bars before dinner. (The only part I would have enjoyed). One day he was so exhausted he consumed 10 Snickers in two days. And still he lost 20 pounds. And hey, he's not a kid. Clearly I'm not the only one impressed. Jim's daily blogs inspired over 100,000 hits.

I have my own story of survival: at age 12, during a visit to Jones Beach in Long Island, I was swept out to sea by what was called a Sea Puss. The thing carried me so far from shore I could barely see any figures on the beach. With no idea what had happened, I believed I was going to die. Yet somehow, with zero hope, I kept swimming. After what seemed hours, the Coast Guard appeared with a 12-man rowboat. And even then, the boat came within inches of crashing into a rock jetty.

This event is described in my latest memoir, *The Tail on my Mother's Kite.*

Somehow the battle to find a publisher now looms large, though by comparison with the above stories it's trivial. As I finished writing 263 letters to agents (16 different versions without getting an agent), I kept thinking about the lady who reminded me it would only be over when I quit.

So I've decided not to quit. But how long should I persist? And how many agent letters should I write? Five hundred? (But no—not that many agents are left.) Direct queries to small publishers? Well, I've sent those … to the few publishers who accept memoirs. And only one answered my query—first with great praise for the manuscript, but ultimately a rejection. (Hence, the blog—"Disappointment isn't Defeat.")

As the chances of success narrow to zero, your focus changes—to a few tiny specks of good news: every agent who read the manuscript said great things about the writing. A few even offered hints about its failings, giving me the chance to make corrections. A dozen friends who read the manuscript loved it, showering me with hope (in spite of knowing friends are supposed to love you).

Well, I've been through this before; as I wrote in an earlier blog, the same scenario occurred with my memoir, *Higher Than Eagles*. After 14 years and three top-notch agents who couldn't convince an editor, I finally found my own traditional publisher.

But hey, things change. If this book takes as long as *Higher Than Eagles*, I'll be beyond giving speeches, I'll be older than Zamperini.

So guess what? I'm trying unconventional stuff. With every New Yorker I meet I say, "In case you know an editor ..." I talk about the project to strangers, hoping I'll meet somebody who knows somebody. I follow every lead ... and sometimes imagine myself resorting to tricks and lies—which I might do, if only I was good at lying.

Okay, there's always self-publishing. But, as a writing friend said, "Self-publishing will always be there. You've gotta keep trying." Well, I am. I am. I am. Every day I'm mining for miracles.

"Perfect" Family Vacations

LIKE FRENCH PIGS ROOTING FOR TRUFFLES, Hollywood knows where to dig for drama. They start with something that's supposed to be perfect, like a family vacation or a marriage, and tell the naked truth. Dangling reality above their computers, screen writers end up with enough poignant or outrageous material to satisfy even Steven Spielberg.

Among those scenes are moments of bizarre comedy. I'm sure Woody Allen would have loved our recent Hawaiian vacation.

Well, actually, so did we. But we had our moments.

Thirteen of us went to the Big Island on Hawaii— and get this: the youngest was nine months, and the oldest was eighty-seven—four generations. Some of us were divinely married, some were simply married, and some weren't married at all. A few had perfect health, some had spotty health, and one had a glioblastoma, a condition so threatening he shouldn't have been there. For that one we brought a wheelchair—and happily never used it.

Okay, Woody Allen here's your material. The setting, you'd have agreed, was ideal: the multi-level Hapuna Hotel near Kona, where breezes blow (or work themselves into minor hurricanes), where the nation's number-one snorkeling beach is right out front, where the meals are gourmet (but don't fit every pocketbook), and where an occasional Asian tourist arrives wearing a breathing mask. (Go figure).

First, the baby: when you're still taking two naps a day and your night ends before dawn, you do not give your parents a perfect vacation. But when you break into a wide grin with the first glimpse of a family member, you definitely add points to your status. And we added points too—by clapping and cheering every time he stood alone.

Health problems should have loomed larger than they did. The family member with a brain tumor might have kept himself and wife at home. Somehow, Brad did fine—walked more than usual, ate full meals, even swam in the ocean. An outsider wouldn't have known. Turns out I was the health headache. The first night I blew apart with inflammation—with a wrist that swelled so obscenely it was the size of a baseball glove (at two a.m., nobody wants to hear you groan.) Luckily, our son, Dr. Chris, was right next door—and had the right medicine.

The girlfriend with a bad cough never slowed down.

One night we played card games—and finally chased away the two disrupters, who preferred slugging down another glass of wine to learning the rules.

The temperature dispute in bedroom A was never

resolved—me, the wife who cherishes air-conditioning versus Rob, the husband who adores a sauna. "We're going to have problems this summer!" he growled, but I left him to simmer in his hot, moisture-dripping air, and went elsewhere—suspecting after 65 years of marriage we'd work out the summer, too.

Meals were a compromise between Cadillac-costly and Chevy-cheap ... the outrageously-priced dinners offset by peanut-butter-and-jelly lunches a la Costco.

As a family, we worked out problems: baby Corbin could have wrecked some dinners, but never did. To accommodate him one night, we moved the entire group into an unused dining room, ordered room service, and let Corbin wander off to dig his fingers into nearby planters. Our group was loud enough to sound like a whole dining room all by ourselves.

Three boxes of Sees Candy could have blown up into a family fracas: instead, two members ate an entire box in one twenty-minute sitting, and the rest of us glanced into the empty box with its drifting wrappers and dolefully shook our heads. Finally our patriarch, Rob, parceled out the other boxes in little dabs.

It was our natural born leader, Tracy, who persuaded us, spur-of-the-moment, to enter the ocean for a group photo op —and never mind that some of us were fully dressed. The picture, with gentle waves lapping around all those fully-clad people, became something of a surprise.

The high point for me was when Dane's girlfriend said in amazement, "You're a big family, but you all get along so well."

Well, we don't always. But we all want to make our big family "work," and so most of the time we do.

Tempest Over Temperature

THE OTHER DAY, LATE JUNE, I CAME DOWNSTAIRS from several hours in my office to find Rob sitting in a sauna. Well, it was our family room, actually, but I could almost see a pile of glowing stones in the corner. It's a wonder the windows weren't fogged up from his over-heated breath. There sat Bob in his chair, oblivious … perfectly content, apparently, that the ceiling fan was still propelling hot vapors over his body.

But the cats not so much. They were lying under the fan, too, their legs splayed out to catch whatever moving air was available—even air that was seemingly straight from an oven.

I stood at the threshold, incredulous. How long had Rob been cooking in his chair? And the cats nearby, all but comatose? When, if ever, was Rob going to make his way to the air-conditioning switch in the next room?

I didn't have to think long. The answer was never.

Rob likes most things hot: Caribbean beaches, cof-fee, his car, and women.

I prefer everything cool or cold—like skiing in Sierra blizzards, where I was often the only idiot still out there, still using the chair lift. For me, bedrooms should be frosty, maybe 55 degrees. (Rob would prefer

80.) Since childhood I've reasoned, You can add extra clothes when it's cold, but how far past your skin can you strip when it's hot?

When it comes to vacations, Rob studies brochures that feature palm trees, tropical seas, and blasting sun, while I read about overcast skies and alpine villages. Usually Rob wins. I once talked him into an Alaskan cruise, thinking "Ah! Sweaters!" But he prevailed anyway. When we arrived, everyone was in sandals and shorts, because Fairbanks was having a heat wave!

How does a marriage accommodate one person who sweats, is constantly wet, and thus remains cool, and the other who doesn't sweat at all and accumulates heat like a black car left in the sun?

Until this summer we mostly accepted what California had to offer—a few cold nights and lots of hot nights. And then we acquired air-conditioning in the bedroom, and our marriage took on a nasty blip. After I turned the air to 70, Rob growled, "I was cold all night. I can see right now—we're going to have a bad summer!"

Oh Lord, I thought, summer in California is forever. By August we'll be divorced. I changed the temperature setting to 74. Neither of us is perfectly happy—but at least we're still sleeping in the same bedroom.

Killers in Our Neighborhood

Nobody imagined we'd ever see this: at 3:00 in the afternoon, a huge gray coyote standing on a backyard wall.

Our daughter, Tracy, lives in a nice neighborhood with yards enclosed by high, impervious block structures. Tracy's niece, Christy, happened to be sitting in the family room when she glanced out the window. "There's a coyote up on your wall," she said calmly.

"What!" Tracy shouted and ran for the door leading to the outside. Her small dog was out in the yard, barking furiously and running toward the wall. Not *away* from it, *toward* it—as though this tiny snack-on-legs could scare away an animal as big and ferocious as a wolf.

Running like the athlete she is, Tracy screamed, threw up her arms, and continued shrieking as she raced toward the intruder. Beside her, Ollie ran too—a black-and-white Cavachon, a virtual movie star of a dog. Clearly, the coyote had a choice between jumping down to grab the movie star, or jumping off in another direction. With Tracy in full-ferocity mode, he chose to leap in the other direction, and disappeared into a neighbor's yard.

With that, Tracy's life changed. Coyote stories poured in—about two coyotes on a remote ranch who grabbed two small dogs and ran off with them. Reacting fast, the rancher shot one of the coyotes, who then dropped its prey. But the other beast, with the pup in his jaws, kept running. They never saw their pet again.

Meanwhile, the ranch owner nursed the injured dog back to life. Once more able to run outside, he was still in danger. A month later, the second coyote came back and got him.

About a year ago, at dusk, I was driving down the largest street near our home when I spotted two huge coyotes trotting along the road ahead of me. I followed them into a cul-de-sac and honked, and the two darted into a neighbor's yard.

I'd forgotten all about them until the disaster on our own street. At dawn, two weeks ago, our neighbor let her dog outside on her driveway to do his morning business. Even as the neighbor watched, a coyote swooped in and grabbed the dog in its teeth. She was devastated.

Now that we know coyotes have a memory, that they operate in pairs and are willing to stalk their prey for however long it takes, that they are not averse to appearing in the daytime, or even with people nearby, Tracy no longer lets Ollie come and go in his own yard. Every two hours she takes her pet outside—on a leash—and she's closed her doggy door for all time.

In one terrible moment, Ollie became a house-bound prisoner. But Tracy is determined to keep him alive. To those who know her current situation, it's clear that losing Ollie would be another disaster, more than she could endure.

Buried Under "Stuff"

The other day I was looking for a receipt on our breakfast room table. I dug around a bit—among travel articles, prescription warnings, university health letters, family clips—and realized it was hopeless. How deep should I dig, anyway? … if, in fact, the thing was even there. Who knew?

Among those who have seen that stack (the table equivalent of a five-car freeway pile-up) are friends who draw benign comfort. *Gee, this looks like one of my tables.* And others, like my daughter, who say nothing but think, *Thank God this isn't mine.*

That day something snapped. *I can't stand this any longer.* With that, I moved pile after pile to the family room couch, and from there I began sorting. As I dug deeper, strata lines appeared, like the color variations that appear in old, sliced-away hills. There they delineate the centuries. With us the lines represented years—damn near decades. One layer had been dunked in spilled coffee. Another was sprinkled with sugar. At the bottom were cocoa stains. The final papers dated back to 2007, replete with invitations to events I couldn't remember. The process resembled an archaeological dig.

Today our table is so clean that one of our grandkids

actually gasped, and now my husband won't let me set down the slightest thing, not even a book.

Which reminds me of other spots in our house … the den where Rob stores calendars dating back to 2011 and piles of *National Geographics* (which even our library won't accept). When do we ever look at any of them?

After last-year's scary backyard fire when we nearly lost the house, the thought occurred to me: if the place burned, how much would I miss? The answer was obvious—not the clothes we never wear, nor the stones we've collected in little dishes, nor the closet with too many towels. We wouldn't care about the old *Reader's Digests* stuffed in a bathroom drawer. Most are long-since forgotten.

We'd mourn only our writings. And the pictures: our two mothers as girls, our children as babies. And maybe some of our clothes, and a few gifts and notes from each other. We might have problems with recent tax records.

But my drawer full of nearly-new purses? Hey, I keep forgetting I even have them.

Which is why, when we go on trips, we donate newspapers to schools. If there's anything I've learned about life, it's that you live it forwards, not backwards. You simply never re-read that article too good to throw away. As many times as you promise yourself, *I'll look at this stuff when I'm old*, the truth is plain: you never get that old.

And now we're heading for a river trip—Budapest to Amsterdam, cruising three classic rivers. In a few weeks I'll doubtless have something new to blog about.

Idiot Engineering

I LOVE AND RESPECT ENGINEERS—MY BROTHER IS one of them—but they seem to come in several flavors: the guys at the top who put men on the moon, and those on lower rungs who are unable to design a public bathroom that makes sense.

Sure, among the populace are a few slobbish females who leave a bathroom stall with nary a backward flush. To counteract these few, engineers have designed self-flushing toilets that respond without input from the user. I've heard them in public places—The Lonely Commodes, toilets in empty stalls, flushing away over and over, flushing themselves hoarse, as though for their own entertainment.

I've had nasty encounters with another variety—the Premature Evacuators. They wait until the seat cover is nicely placed, then flush away the cover just as you're unzipping your pants. Many a time I've heard a suspicious noise and whirled around, throwing my palms onto the seat to save the cover. These are the potties that demand you use them without wasting time pulling down your trousers.

I've met the Nervous Flushers—the ones that sail into action two or three times, just for the hell of it, before you leave the stall.

Why, we wonder, did engineers decide ninety-nine percent of women couldn't be trusted? That we were somehow unwilling to press down that all-important handle? For one … and yes, only one, flush?

A few engineer-designed sinks are no better. Okay, water is precious and needs to be conserved. We get it. So they give you cold water that runs only when your hands are soaped and under the faucet. (I'm okay with that). But in some bathrooms the sink offers only mini-squirts of water, not enough in one squirt to rinse one well-lathered hand, let alone two. For those I've had to retreat and advance my fingers seven or eight times, and in the end achieved maybe eight teaspoons of liquid— meaning the rest of the soap had to be wiped away on a paper towel.

And speaking of towels. Why did so many bath-room designers position the paper towels across the room from the sinks … leaving us no recourse but to drip, drip, drip, on the way to drying off? Who, pray tell, mops the slippery gap between sinks and towels?

Maybe things are different in men's bathrooms. I'll never know. But I do have one suggestion—that women engineers design the equipment for women's bathrooms. Why on earth was this job entrusted to someone who, on most occasions, needs only one downward zip and one grab and he's good to go?

P.S. I WAS REMINDED TODAY THAT DUBIOUS ENGIneering is not confined to bathrooms. Kirkland's delicious "complete nutrition shake" comes with an attached straw—which is too short for the container. When you poke it into the hole, the straw drops into the liquid and disappears. You wonder—who thought this was a good idea?

And Emily's List (which I love), provides a return envelope which is too small for the material they want sent back. No matter how you fold them, the sheets don't fit.

Last, but certainly not least—an article about cell phones declares that if you let them drop too often to zero, soon the battery will be so weak it won't rouse enough to take a charge. (At the moment, mine is practically comatose). On the other hand, phones do best, they say, when charged to only 60 or 80 percent. So I ask ... what nerd hovers over his charging phone to pull the plug at exactly 80 percent? For that, you'd have to set your alarm for 2:00 a.m.

I'd buy a new phone—except I'm waiting for one that holds a charge for ... how about two whole days?

The Saddest of Ironies

The *Los Angeles Times* headline came out one day before it happened to us: "Making a date with death."

Everybody had heard about it—the 29-year-old woman who moved to Oregon so she could choose her last weeks, then her own very last day. Brittany Maynard had stage-four brain cancer and wanted to die in her own way on a date of her own choosing. A group called Compassion and Choices supported her—and even more, advocates for this right in other states.

There was no choice in my daughter's house.

For a year, almost to the day, Brad's brain tumor had its way in his life and in Tracy's, dictating that he would never again drive a car, that an eleven-hour surgery would cost him significant loss of eyesight and speech, and that Tracy would be his full-time nurse—with yes, some amazing help from an angel, Lorena, whom she found in the last month. A multitude of friends also helped—with more dinners and visits and outpourings of love than any of us could have imagined. Tracy's friends and family and Lorena literally sustained her.

Still, the year was Tracy's to live through, and neither Brad nor Tracy could dictate any of it—how long he'd be able to walk, when speech would utterly desert him, whether he would end up spending nearly two months in bed, unable to leave, and mostly unable to eat or move.

One day after the headline, last night in fact, our family's agony ended. And in her own way, Tracy brought Brad the best death possible—with a young man, an intern from Brad's company, playing a guitar and singing the kind of music Brad loved—for a solid two hours, until Brad took the last of several deep breaths. Some of this was accidental—until the last part of the day nobody even knew that Anthony played the guitar, or that, like James Taylor, he had such a sweet singing voice. Once we discovered his talents, Tracy begged him to keep playing, and he did.

Everybody has his own opinion of Brittany Maynard's decision—and even now, I'm not sure I would have chosen such an abrupt ending for Brad. During that year he had a few relatively decent months—able to walk his daughter down the aisle, even take two family trips. But the last few months ... those were a lifetime that were better cut short. Hospice helped—but not enough. Brad sometimes held a finger to his head—playfully?—Indicating he would shoot himself.

California has no answers, at least none that are legal. Perhaps we need a few.

The Hole in Our Lives

While I was overcome, at first, by the circumstances of my son-in-law's death (so recent and so raw), the important message was left unsaid: *What about his life?*

His dying may be over, but in strange ways, maybe not so strange, Brad Hagen's life soldiers on. As Tracy says, "He was a powerful presence."

Brad was the ultimate foodie. "You'll be in Minneapolis?" he'd say to someone about to take a trip (or Detroit, or Boston, or Dallas or even Nowheresville), "I know this little restaurant, off the main drag, hard to find, only the locals know about it, but the food is extraordinary." And you'd go there and the sausages, or pancakes, or soups or whatever would be delicious …

The best thing Brad's mother did for him was to cook good meals. She turned her cooking into love, and love in turn became food. In the best sense, Brad became a gourmet. But he was always an appreciator. "Hey, Tracy, you've done a great job with this squash, it's good!"

While he never ate too much, Brad tasted everything, and you had to get used to seeing his fork creeping into your plate. With him, you never went to chain restaurants; instead he found all the odd little Mom and

Pops hiding next to hardware stores, or behind box out-lets—and if he didn't exactly dictate what you ordered, he tried to, and if you defied him, he'd turn resigned, even crestfallen—but then you'd see his fork coming your way.

In his work as a videographer, Brad was world class. To see him behind a camera was to appreciate what it means to take the ultimate photos, to capture the best images that perfect lighting, exact camera angles, and well-considered background can produce. His clients, among them CEOs of major companies, understood how good he was. And the topper was always the rec-ommended restaurant that came later.

It was extraordinary the way Brad invariably wel-comed Rob and me to come over for meals, gracious-ly and without question; in my heart I never stopped thanking him—or Tracy, either. After dinner we played games, and never mind that we two wordsmiths taught him our best word game, Boggle, fully expecting to win.

Within a month Brad was beating us, figuring out ways to extend simple words into long, point-winning answers. As always I found myself sputtering, "Can you believe this, Rob? He's won again!"

Brad didn't gloat. He just smiled.

Thanks to the imbalance in his own parenting—an especially kind father—his feelings toward Rob and me were lopsided. I never minded that every time I arrived at his house, his first words were, "Where's Rob?" Kind of funny, really. But if I needed help on anything, technical or non technical, he jumped in without question.

Nothing reveals character and skills more than a family trip. Alone among us, Brad was a miracle packer, able to fit too much luggage into too little taxi space … like Houdini. The rest of us never helped, we just stood around and gaped.

The most important statement about Brad comes last. When he married Tracy, he also married her two young children, Dane, 13, and Jamie, 16. Within a few years both of them, by their own choice, were calling him Dad. You can't say more about a man than that.

Clearly, Brad has left a big hole in all our lives.

The Captain's Jacket

Extraordinary Moments on a Riverboat Cruise

WE GUESSED IT WOULD BE THIS WAY—THAT TRACY would find she couldn't bear to take our family river trip without Brad … that she'd choose instead to leave town for a "woman's weekend away" with old and dear friends. And after that she'd fly to Texas to play in a long-planned tennis tournament. We weren't surprised to learn, later, that she broke down on the plane and found herself sobbing.

I wished I'd been with her.

We supposed as well that our river-cruising adventures on a Tauck Tour would be better planned, less commercial, and more fun than most other tours.

Our last prediction was based on an adventure thirty years ago, when Rob and I were part of a Tauck Tour heli-hiking trip, dropped off by whirlybirds for a series of hikes through Canada's Caribou mountains. As travelers allergic to regimentation, Rob and I were astonished at Tauck's light touch. In fact we found the adventure so enjoyable we did it twice—the second time with Tracy and he first husband, Geoff.

But does anything stay the same?

Apparently some things do; for us, this last month, the light touch continued. Traveling by Tauck river boat along the Danube, Main, and Rhine rivers from Budapest to Amsterdam, we could visit, at no added cost, all the castles, churches, museums and shops available to tourists. For a few we were taken a short distance by bus, but for most the ship's guides led us on walking tours, straight from the ship through nearby cobblestone streets. (Alternatively, we could stay on board and loaf.)

For Rob and me, an extraordinary moment came early. The second day I decided the crew wore such good-looking jackets, I wanted to buy one. Rob and I were in the ship's small boutique, looking through garments, when I realized the ship had sold out of the classy ones I'd seen on staff. At that moment, a very tall, very handsome man wandered into the area. With no idea who he was, I took one look, pointed, and said with a grin, "*There's* the jacket I want!"

The man heard me. Without a moment's hesitation, he shrugged his way out of the garment and handed it to me, mumbling under his breath that I might want to get it washed. I could hardly believe what he'd done. I stood there holding the jacket, struck dumb with surprise, but also thrilled. I was thinking,

You certainly didn't need to do that!

At that moment I happened to look closer and saw the I.D. badge pinned to his shirt. The amazing gentleman was none other than Patrick Tietz, the ship's captain. If I'd been surprised before, now I was breathless with astonishment. *The captain has just given me his jacket!* A few words of thanks hardly seemed adequate.

For the rest of the day I couldn't stop telling the story. Someone said, "I bet you'll wear it a lot," and I said, "I may sleep in it."

Notable moments kept coming. A few nights later, Rob and I decided the ship's musician was playing such great music we had to get up and dance. When no one joined us, we felt obligated to give it our all, even Rob with his cane. At the end, all the spectators clapped. In a moment of celebration, Rob raised his cane, gave a great triumphant wave ... and broke the chandelier.

Above our heads, glass cascaded down onto the floor. Neither of us could believe what he'd done. We were mortified, red-faced. To bursts of laughter, we crept back to our seats. Next day crew members were on ladders fixing the enormous overhead lights, and a passenger remarked, "Oh, you're the couple that brought down the house."

Tauck didn't charge us for the breakage—or anything else. You might say the only expense was to our bodies—the one or two miles we ended up walking each day. Once again, Rob and I did our bit, Rob with his cane, me taking deep breaths. And lo—our three big meals each day did not add a single pound.

As a family of six (two sons and their wives), we kept attracting unexpected attention. One night we won the ship's trivia contest. Another night a paper napkin on our table fell across a candle, and within seconds all the napkins around us were aflame. As we beat out flames, the announcer stopped talking and said, "I see we've got a little fire here."

Two more nights our group again won the Trivia contests ... once because the judges asked for original ways to convey the answers and, among some clever maneuvers by Kenny, Chris flew our response in on a paper airplane.

By prior arrangement with Tauck, I gave an afternoon speech on the topic, "Do you want to write a memoir?" which brought me new friends ... and readers who ordered my e-books while still aboard the ship.

Tauck paid for everything—including ship's bicycles for the everyday use of Kenny and Melanie, Chris and Betty-Jo (they rode through most towns), all the shore excursions, three meals a day (whether on or off the boat), tips for the staff, even cocktails and wine at meals. We arrived home with most of our money still in our pockets. Best of all, we came back with the glitter of gold-leaf in castles and churches still affixed to memory.

On another level, we suspect more than a few people will remember us.

Toward the end I realized: *I can't wait to get back to Tracy.*

THE KITCHEN MONSTER

WE NEEDED A NEW TOASTER, OKAY? TO REPLACE our two-slicer that each day figures out anew how it will approach our bread. One day, doubtless after a hard night, it can't rouse itself to fire up all its elements, so it browns each slice on one side only … or, alternatively, it browns one piece and ignores the other. Or sometimes, in an ebullient spirit, it keeps browning until it burns. Trouble is, like a teenager with moods, you never know what you'll get.

Before we got around to buying something better, Tracy inherited a lot of Diner's Club gift points from her husband. "What do you need?" she asked, gracious as always.

"A toaster!" I cried. "With four slots."

"Well," she said as she looked over the catalog, "here's one." And then in a softer tone. "It also cooks eggs."

This I couldn't imagine. But I told her to order it anyway.

Yesterday it came. So let me paint the picture. For two-thirds of its length, this appliance is just a four-slice toaster. But then the last third sports two little frying pans that stick out into space, apropos of nothing, except that the pans also have lids and non-removable, further-protruding knobs, making it a ship that grew too big for its berth.

At the moment the thing is sitting on my drain board like an obese, but shiny squatter, taking up so much space I can hardly cook around it. It's waiting to be placed elsewhere, somewhere permanent—which won't happen until I dismantle a big chunk of the kitchen. As I work, I keep giggling, and from across the room Bob hears me and says, "What were they THINKING?"

As I push it aside, discovering there's actually no-where for it to go, I keep picturing what went on in the boardroom of West Bend. "You want to invent WHAT?" the president asks, and the inventor says earnestly, "Who wouldn't want a cooks-all appliance?" and board members shake their heads and one says, "Not MY wife," but the president finally says, "Well, we've got some development money. Give it a try."

"Twenty-thousand dollars okay?" the inventor asks, to which the daring president answers, "Why not twenty-thousand?" Then, as my grandson says, "They never did much field testing."

I can tell you what happened next. Having found no takers among normal retail, West Bend was saddled with five-thousand "gifts"—which they pawned off on Diner's Club. And Diner's Club is currently left with four-hundred and ninety-nine, because we have the other one.

Even Rob, who tries to find a spot for everything, can't figure out its placement. The only reasonable scenario (egg pans facing the wall) would leave the controls buried against our refrigerator. Egg-pans-out, means I'd have to reach over the little darlings to get at the toaster slots. We are currently engaged in a typical Wills debate. "Let's make it a humorous white elephant," I say, and Bob says grimly, "It's an elephant, all right—but I intend to keep it."

So now I'm asking the world. Is there anyone out there who wants a toaster that also cooks eggs?

Speak up. I can't hear you.

The Tail on my Mother's Kite

WHAT CAN POSSIBLY GO WRONG IN A HOUSEHOLD led by a mother who is rich, beautiful, and educated at Smith college?

As my brother, Allan, and I learned, the answer is everything. Thanks to our mother, who eventually married seven times, we were dragged from city to city and husband to husband. Yet I suppose this memoir proves that if kids are resilient enough they can survive almost anything.

It was truly a crazy childhood. At times we grasped we were like suitcases that became too heavy to carry; at those moments our mother simply dumped us off to live with strangers. She wasn't intentionally cruel—but clearly, when her own problems rose up and stifled her, Allan and I became her two inconvenient children.

For the past two years I've relived an era where children sometimes had to push cars to make them run, where we kids entertained ourselves with Monopoly because movies and radio were the only outside diversions, and where country people like us lived on unpaved roads—and somehow, trudging a mile to the school bus, Allan and I walked uphill both ways.

Here, then, is the first page from *The Tail on My*

Mother's Kite.

AFTER THE FIRE, NOTHING WAS EVER THE SAME.

Even to our mother who, like Elizabeth Taylor, was destined by her own choice to have seven husbands, nothing was more life-changing than the Siskiyou County forest fire.

Like a cougar stalking its prey, the fire crept down the ridges of Mount Eddy and arrived in full destruction mode at our family's virgin guest ranch, a 320-acre property with two houses—one wrinkled and old, the other newly framed, barely roofed. The year was 1939.

In the distance Mount Shasta still rose above the clouds, lofty and gleaming white, disdainful in its splendor as though such devastation a mere seven miles away was beneath its notice.

Unlike the grownups, I hadn't seen the fire coming. As I stood in the dirt road with our mile-away neighbors, I watched in awe as one by one, flames shot up the pines on a distant hill. We'd never seen anything like it. In unison, Alice Deetz and her three boys and I all shouted, "Oooh! There's another one!" "Oh … wow!" "A big one! Look at that!" We were spectators at a shocking, living event, thrilled but not afraid. The sparking hill was far away, across a vast meadow—as all of us knew, in its own universe.

I thought, *Wait 'til I tell people about this! They won't*

believe what I'm seeing.

For readers who wish to continue, the book is available on Amazon—or you can buy it, autographed, on my web site: *Maralys.com*

From Promenade Circle to Suicide Ledge

Before Rob and I left the elevator, I knew we were in trouble.

I'd somehow forgotten that Rob had bought our concert tickets as a "bargain." Our stubs said, "Promenade Circle," which had such a nice, friendly ring to it that I assumed our seats in Segerstrom Hall would be in some kind of relaxed, roomy area, where theater-goers actually found enough space and time to stroll. Which is why Rob and I kept jumping off the elevator at successive floors—only to have a fellow rider assure us this was not yet the promenade level. Finally the lady said with a smile, "Promenade is in the nosebleed section."

I looked at her and blinked. "Oh," I said. But I was thinking, *At least we're in Row A, which is usually a good thing.*

As it turned out, not always.

When we finally landed at Promenade, an usher pointed us to a door … and there we saw Row A—about ninety-three tiers up from Orchestra, and suspended out in space. Literally. And Row A tighter than the cheapest row in Spirit Airlines, jammed right up against its neighbor—in this case, the world's worst excuse for a rail.

Between us and our seats were several dozen patrons, all hunkered down. The space between their various knees and the thigh-high rail (well, that's how high it appeared), was maybe six inches. After a quick glance, I said, "Let's just stay here, Rob. Somewhere on the edge." I tried to back away.

Then a voice whispered, "There's someone coming in right behind you," and to my horror, I was forced to squeeze my way past knees and shoes, past people who wouldn't budge an inch ... every second hideously aware that if I stumbled or faltered I'd go right over that tiny little rail to my death.

The farther I went, the more it appeared we'd be parked at the top of a broken roller coaster, in the two most precarious spots in the house. Thanks to the curve of the tier, we'd be hanging out more than anyone else, with only inches between us and well ... a ten-thousand-foot drop. With pounding heart, I sat down fast, and so did Rob. But getting seated provided no comfort.

I looked around and could hardly breathe. I've never been afraid of heights, but suddenly I was. There was nothing in front of us but endless space, and that damned, useless little rail. Down below, miles away, Beethoven began. But who, up here, could listen?

What if there's an earthquake? I wondered. *Why won't my heart stop pounding? What if I have a heart attack, how will they get me out?* I kept telling myself to think about something else, or I'd definitely succumb to a coronary.

Why can't I look down? Well, I can't … I can't look down, I can't. And so it went. Right through the first two movements, until Rob gave me a little poke and whispered, "Watch the percussionist."

So I watched the percussionist beating his drums. *Keep beating,* I thought. *Get it over with.* But then my thoughts strayed. *How will we get out at intermission— past all those stubborn people? What if we topple over the edge?*

I kept telling myself: STOP THINKING.

Finally Beethoven blasted into silence. Rob slowly rose. Moving like a turtle, he edged past those still seated … and very carefully I followed, inch by inch. *Oh God,* I thought as we left the ledge. *Oh, Dear Heaven,* we're out *of there! We made it!*

Rob said grimly, "We're going down to a lower floor," and I said, "Oh, yes. All the way down, okay? The bottom floor," and he said, "Fine. The bottom floor." So we took the elevator and finished our escape. Still shaken, we stood in the lobby and shared our thoughts.

For once neither of us considered getting in the snack line. "As we headed to our seats," Rob said, "I thought I was going to pass out. I'm dizzy enough already. I nearly told you, Grab me, Babe, if I start to wobble." I nodded. He said, "I was also thinking, If I'm unconscious, how will they get me out?" I nodded again. "After we sat, I was thinking, What if there's an earthquake? I decided we'd better distract ourselves and watch the percussionist ... Then I thought, In an earthquake we'd fall farther than anyone." He added, "Right on those people a mile away—down in orchestra."

I told him my version—same as his. "It's a wonder *anyone* sits there," I said. "I won't go back. Ever. No one can make me. Not for ten thousand dollars."

He nodded. "Nor I." He shook his fingers. "Funny how we each figured we were going to die—me with a deadly faint, you with a heart attack." We turned to each other and exchanged nods.

After awhile I looked around. "We have to go somewhere, Rob, for the second half. Let's see if our regular seats are open." And Praise Heaven, they were. First level, two best seats in the house.

Next to us was a couple who couldn't wait to make a comment. The man pointed skyward. "We just escaped from up there."

"So did we," I said, and we both rolled our eyes.

So there in our good seats we watched a virtuoso pound the piano through Rachmaninoff's 2nd piano concerto, so close I could see the pianist's expressive, music-loving face, and I thought, *I adore that man ...* Then I thought as I squeezed Rob's knee, *We listened to this together at Stanford, and isn't this the greatest music in the world? And wow! We're both here … it's heaven … and we're alive!*

Long Silences and Hurt Feelings

It's Christmas and I'm thinking of writing a conciliatory letter. Two of my friends have had "words"—well, actually, they've blown up at each other—and it seems to me a few thoughts from an outsider might help. That is, if I'm allowed to write such a letter.

With only a little looking around, any of us can become an expert on the awful damage done by hurt feelings and long silences. Sometimes the ripped-up and torn-apart places and bitterness go with the person to her grave—a heart that hurts until it finally stops beating. And for what purpose?

One of my friends didn't speak to her son for 21 years. When they finally reconciled, they must have been asking themselves, "Why didn't we do this years ago?" What does it take, really, to do a little compassionate exploring into another's dark feelings and bring them to the surface? And then apply a touch of salve?

If nations can do it, why can't we as individuals?

Think of the magical Christmas eve in World War I, where Germans and Brits stopped fighting for one night and stepped into no-man's land and sang carols together … and how that moment still takes our breath away. And yet the war went on. Why couldn't they stretch out that night ... well, indefinitely?

Think of Cuba. What purpose was served in fifty years of shunning—no despising—that country and its dictator, with no sign that anything would change? Ever? Why did we let it go on so long? Us turning our backs on them, and them both jealous of and furious with us? Surely, when we reach across the abyss in any way—with our computers, our Cuisinarts, our cars—and finally with our people—the bitterness will fade.

And China ... it took Richard Nixon, a bitter man himself, to open a door that has since remained open. Granted, China does not emulate or value some of what we treasure in a democracy—but hey, we're speaking to them, we're trading with them, we're swapping citizens back and forth. Which is a tad better than swapping bombs.

Then there's North Korea ... remember when our New York Philharmonic orchestra played a concert over there? Remember the clapping, the smiles, the hand-shakes, the hugs? Some of us are asking—when can we do it again?

Remember the best thing our country ever did? We adapted the Marshall Plan. We used our citizens' tax money to rehabilitate Germany. Then, thanks to MacArthur, we also helped Japan—the two countries we'd just been fighting. Has any program ever worked better to restore peace in the world than those amazing decisions?

In our family one of us does not apologize. Ever. It's just the way it is. As a young, occasionally-embattled bride, I tried not speaking to him—once for a day and a half. And frankly, I couldn't stand it. So now when we fight, and occasionally we still do, I'm the one who forces my voice into normal tones and speaks first. It's not fair and it hurts my pride and usually it galls me.

But I'd rather speak first than not speak at all. I'd rather live with him than live without him. It turns out my happiness comes at a price—I'm the one who has to proffer the initial note of truce, which I can only do by resolving once again that pride is less important than peace.

The Magic of Music, the Bounty of Books

When we got out of bed this morning, Rob and I did not know we were headed for Carnegie Hall. We thought we were going to a neighbor's house about four blocks away. "I'll get my coffee up there," he said, and I said, "Aren't we lucky that we can roll out of the covers and we're practically there?"

And so it was once again. My membership in Town and Country, a support group for the Orange County Philharmonic, had brought us another musical event—nearby, in our friend's house. Twenty minutes later, with coffee and rolls on a plate beside us, Rob and I were listening to Adela Kwan, a 32-year-old virtuoso pianist, and Priyanka Venkatesh, 27, a violinist whose music literally soared. Her final piece was Bach, a 15-minute solo played without a score, but with such magic our group was mesmerized.

I sat there thinking, *I've been a serious writer for forty years, yet I don't have the words to describe what she's doing.* All those memorized notes—often two of them played at once and in harmony. And with such poetry, such rich, emotional overtones. She was beautiful as well, as she stood there swaying to her violin's music. Rob and I were silently adoring. Besides the fact she'd been concertmaster in numerous orchestras (such as at Stanford), and was now pursuing a doctorate in music at UCI, she could have been a headliner anywhere, in the world's most illustrious concert halls.

We could easily picture her at the Kennedy Center.

But here she was—here were the two of them—four blocks from our home.

Afterwards, amid nearly nonstop clapping, I ran to the car for copies of *The Tail on My Mother's Kite*. Would the young women like them? I wondered. It didn't matter, this was the best I could give. And one for the hostess, too.

And yes, they did like them. In fact all three appeared thrilled.

On the way home I said, "These books will never make me rich ... but each time I give one as a gift I *feel* rich. For that reason alone, I'm glad I wrote them."

Rob smiled. "You go on feeling rich, Babe. I'll go on feeding us."

What Wealth Does to Your Soul

Until now, I've never been aware that wealth does *anything* to your soul.

But the magazine, *The Week* (December 31, 2014), has given us this title, having found some amazing evidence about morality and wealth. I was instantly fascinated, having never been aware that being rich had consequences. Perhaps it's because we're simply not that wealthy—meaning until now our souls have remained unafflicted.

The sub-title reads: "Getting rich won't make you happy," said Michael Lewis, "but it will make you more selfish and dishonest." Of course from then on I was hooked.

The article cites numerous studies, beginning with one about rich kids at a tennis camp—and how the director used a shortage of the "best" cereal—Fruit Loops—to teach kids that rushing to grab the preferred cereal made them feel worse than backing off and leaving it for some other kid. For those children, the tennis camp became a life lesson on the good feelings inspired by generosity. Beautifully written, this study will remain in memory—a microcosm of the best and worst in all of us.

Close to these same ideas, I can share a few

experiences of my own. My family won't like my bringing this up, but since I've written a book titled, *Save My Son*, it's no secret that we have a son with addiction problems. And thus it should come as no surprise that from time to time we've visited him in our local jail. Some days it was miserably hot and the outside line was long, and I was forced to stand there with everyone else, feeling out of place and not "one of the crowd."

Yet the same thing happened over and over: just as I'd reached some kind of nadir of snobbishness and misery, some woman or man who was "not my people," would lean toward me and say, "Why don't you go sit down over there?" pointing to a cement bench. "I'll save your place in line." This happened to me many times—a moment of generosity extended by someone of a different race and social class. In fact, I can honestly say I've found more kindness in jail lines than any other kind of line.

It happened again a few nights ago. Rob and I were having hamburgers at *In and Out*, squeezed together at a tiny table that passed for a booth. Next to us was a lady we'd never have met at Stanford. Yet she was clearly worried about us. "Over there," she said suddenly, "there's a table that's come empty," and she urged us to go grab it. When somebody else took it first, she never stopped searching—to help us.

Would we have done this for somebody else?

Probably not.

The article includes a study that showed it was the expensive cars that were four times more likely to cut in front of other vehicles than the cheap ones—and far less likely to respect the rights of pedestrians. Another study of truly rich people found that most declared they'd need two to three times more money to feel happier. A researcher explains what actually happens to the very rich—in biological terms. You should read the article for yourself.

We are now of an age where our kids and grandkids can't think of what to give us for Christmas—and we don't blame them. Rob and I are out of ideas for what to give each other. But I can say—I hope with humility—that my happiest moment each year comes when Rob decides to give our ten grandkids some common stock. Just knowing what it means to them, to their modest way of life, lights up my soul.

A Simple Country We Once Loved

EVERY WEEK THE PAPERS CARRY GRIM STORIES about Mexico—students abducted and beheaded. Towns protecting themselves with vigilantes in lieu of policemen. Bus loads of tourists waylaid—and if they're lucky, released.

Let me tell you about our adventures in Mexico—a once simple, but gay and carefree country that now seems to have vanished. Rob and I first went there when we were young, with three little boys at home. We began in Mazatlan, where we rented bicycles and pedaled around the countryside. For me, in my cute white shorts, the whoo, whoo whistling from men in cars, from guys working along the road, made me feel ... well, young and beautiful.

On one steep neighborhood street, Rob rode ahead and left me pedaling valiantly, trying to make it up the hill. Suddenly a man came running out of a nearby house. Alarmed, I got off my bike and waited. But he signaled me to get back on. To my huge surprise, he found a spot for his hands and pushed me all the way to the top. We waved to each other as he left. It was then that kind of country.

The primitive aspects made good stories—out

behind one of the best hotels in Mazatlan, we saw someone filling bottles of "agua purificada" … with a hose.

While we drank no water, *something*, some germ or other, reached my insides, and I was suddenly confined to our hotel bed, feverish and worse. With Rob determined to explore further south, after one day of letting me lie, he approached the bed. "Get up, Babe," he urged, "you'll be fine."

I couldn't believe he was serious. But apparently I was better than I thought, and managed to stagger to my feet. Blinded by the outside sun, I followed him to a reasonably modern bus headed south for Tepec, and then, with a seaward turn, toward the tiny village of San Blas.

The miniature town of San Blas was quaint, but now in summer, almost tourist-free … though its hotel, right on the beach was, as Rob said, "an exotic destination." Yet the ocean water that far south was so warm it was like stepping into a Jacuzzi, much too hot for swimming. Dinner that night was delicious—if you ignored the crabs scuttling between your shoes, or the fact that pigs wandered loose in the kitchen.

In the middle of the night, I awoke with cold sores so painful I couldn't go back to sleep—blisters that covered the lower half of my face and defined the rest of our trip. Next day we departed on another bus—this one so rickety it had boards for seats, and passengers carrying live chickens. The ancient engine smoked and sputtered and threatened any minute to quit.

As we left town, we noticed a man working atop a telephone pole. To our horror, the pole suddenly leaned alarmingly, and with no warning crashed to the ground. The bus went on. Rob and I were shaken, knowing we'd just seen an innocent man die. And nobody around to care.

Back in Mazatlán, we found a kind druggist who stared in horror at my cold sores and prescribed a salve that made no difference. For our next few restaurant meals, we chose seats in back, where I sat with my hand covering my face; I wasn't fit to be seen. But worse, the pain was horrendous.

The man who piloted our plane back to Tijuana was, at heart, a dive bomber. From a level position he suddenly dipped the plane downward, and for long minutes we headed straight for the ground—with passengers moaning and shrieking. At the last second he leveled out and we landed. Amazingly, we hadn't crashed. Come to think of it, that flight was anything but benign.

As we drove north, the official who stopped us at the border took one look at me and shook his head. "Cold sores," Rob explained.

"I've never seen cold sores like that," the man said sympathetically, and he must have wondered if the Americana was bringing back a dread disease. Well, I was and I wasn't. The blisters took a week to disappear—but what didn't disappear were memories of a warm and caring people, and adventures we couldn't duplicate anywhere else.

Sadly, thanks to drugs and cartels, that same trip would now be impossible. Rob and I might still be willing to court adventure—but we'd never take a chance on outright, life-threatening danger.

Maybe I Read Too Much

Occasionally, like this morning, I wake up feeling depressed over man's inhumanity to man. Weeks ago separatists in Ukraine shot down a Malaysian airliner, an act so dreadful it defies belief. Imagine how you'd feel sitting in your airplane seat as the walls around you suddenly fall off?

Particularly poignant was the woman who stood in the Amsterdam airport holding her baby. "I missed the plane," she said. "I've been given a second life." But what about the 298 people who didn't miss the plane?

And today Israel is bringing tanks into Palestine—having yesterday bombed their neighbors' beaches, killing three little boys innocently playing by the water. And Hamas is stupid enough to keep firing rockets into Israel. How can you not conclude that vast numbers of people feel alive only when they're fighting and killing others?

Last night's special on television showed the combined meanness and stupidity of Hitler, how he pigheadedly built tanks so strong they were totally invulnerable to attack—yet were so huge and cumbersome that they were useless, because they couldn't go anywhere.

Even in our country we have so much meanness and stupidity it's hard to read the newspaper. One of the country's biggest retail chains is owned by a family of billionaires—but its workers earn so little per hour they can't buy sufficient food, meaning they only survive with the help of food stamps.

Currently our Congress has refused to pass every bill the president proposes, whether for a slight increase in the minimum wage or background checks for guns (even after 21 Newtown school children were killed by a mad gunman), or equal pay for women—yet the House leader is now suing the president … for what? Because our president yearns to get something accomplished?

Of course all of Iraq is now a hellhole, thanks mostly to a former president who decided to invade that country—as we learned later, for nothing. But he did get a few people killed—over 4000 Americans and some 100,000 Iraqis. If his goal was population control, worldwide, he certainly succeeded.

Well, enough. Outside my window the sun shines and Liquidamber leaves glisten in the light. It's quiet, too. No guns, nobody screaming. Our immediate family, now extended to 10 grandkids and 11 great grandkids and lots of new spouses, is mostly peaceful. We often travel together, in what can only be called a mob, and for the most part we make plenty of noise, but it's good noise. Lots of laughter. Much kidding back and forth. Nobody fighting, no one backbiting.

I guess I should hole up, like a mole, and be grateful

for my world and simply ignore the larger universe. Turn off the TV, cancel the newspapers and pretend all is well. As it is, I relish the few bits of human kindness displayed at the ends of certain news broadcasts, like *On the Road* with Steve Hartman. Maybe the answer, instead, is to turn on the television for a few limited moments—the last segment of ABC. That way, like *Alice in Wonderland*, it's possible to live in a curious but wholly fictitious universe.

Billie Elliott Made Me Cry

I MUST BE LIVING IN A CAVE, LIKE THAT JAPANESE soldier on Guam who hid out until years after World War II was over—because until last week I'd never heard of the story, *Billie Elliott.* Meanwhile, everyone else seemed to know about him and his dramatic tale, and I gathered they'd known for years.

Oh well. Just as our La Mirada tickets were coming up, Rob explained. "It's about a kid whose dad wants him to be a boxer—while he wants to be a ballet dancer."

"Oh," I said, and decided right then I'd probably like the show better than Rob would. Which didn't turn out to be true.

We took our grandson and his wife (who also knew the story) … except none of us could have predicted we'd be getting a jarring surprise.

Before the curtain rose, the show's producer, Tom McCoy, came out and explained that their young star had practiced until his part was polished to perfection … then last Saturday, one week before opening, the boy had been doing a last-scene dance, and somehow landed wrong and broke his arm.

Tom motioned to a down-front seat. "Stand up, Noah Parets," and the boy did, and sure enough, there he was, with his arm in a sling.

Tom McCoy went on. "We got lucky. We found another young man who lives in Florida, and he'd done the show in the United States and in London, and he came out to fill in for us. We think you'll be surprised."

Surprised was the wrong word. Mitchell Tobin was a phenomenon. Slight of build and not very tall, Mitchell was fourteen, but appeared about twelve—with an appealing face that made him look like a kid who wouldn't exactly take to boxing. Yet he was all boy, and it didn't seem likely he'd be eager to wear a tutu, either. He was just a young kid who wanted to dance … charming, breathless, innocent, and an actor who, in a British accent, talked to his "dead" mother on stage in ways that brought tears to our eyes.

But his dancing … how many fourteen-year-olds can do twenty toe spins in a row, or soar through the air like an eagle, with arms and legs positioned in exotic ballet poses?

How many can appear they'd been dancing for longer than their years on earth? Yet this boy did. He spun, he did beautiful space flips, he jumped and dashed elegantly—at the end bringing the audience to their feet with cheers and prolonged clapping.

None of us could believe it. He must have had, at most, five days to practice in this strange city—for him an all-new cast, a new stage, a new director. Yet somehow the pieces went together flawlessly … with emotions so poignant that I wasn't the only one with tears in her eyes.

Next day when I read the review in the *Los Angeles Times* "Calendar", they agreed with everything I'd been thinking about that amazing young man from Florida.

How my Grandfather Made it to America

Stuttgart, Germany. February 8, 1869.

FOR A COLD EVENING IN THE WOODED SECTION OF Stuttgart, the German wedding had an unusual aura of warmth and good cheer. Outside, the falling snow was quiet, relentless. But inside the biergarten—all stone and brick—the yellow-painted walls reflected back the heat of the revelers. Above their heads, alpine horns, antlered elk heads and multi-colored local flags lined the walls, adding to an air of festivity.

Surrounded by male friends, Christian Ludwig Heinrich Klumpp held up his beer stein to salute them. "Ach! I will soon lose my freedom!" he sang out, but one of them shouted back, "Jah! But you vill once more test your manhood!" and with that, the group roared.

Nearby, Margaretha Schnieder, sheltered within a cluster of women attendants, blushed in chagrin. So it was known everywhere then—that Heinrich had once spread his masculinity throughout the village.

With the eyes of the revelers upon her, Margaretha straightened proudly. *He is mine,* she thought, *and all his carousing is now over.* She patted the skirt of her white, batiste gown. *From this day forward, Heinrich will not dare be found in any bed except mine.*

Outside, the church bells rang, casting solemn notes into the icy February air. Soon accordion music from within the beer garden seeped out through cracks around the window and joined the church bells in song. A wedding was always a fine reason to combine one kind of note with another.

THE KNOCK ON MARGARETHA'S DOOR SEEMED innocent enough, though wholly unexpected. Heavy with child, she responded calmly to the midday tap on her oaken door, surprised to see the woman who stood outside. The Frau's black hair was pulled straight back, and her face, once comely, was now a mask of fatigue combined with stolid German determination. A small boy in short pants stood at her side.

"Yes?" Margaretha asked.

The woman didn't hesitate. Lifting the boy's arm, she said, "This is my child, Karl—the son of Heinrich. An unexpected event ... so it's likely Heinrich does not know. But see? He's the image of your husband."

"You and ... Heinrich?" Margaretha stared down at the child, the shock registering on her face, turning her pale.

"I am Rosina Wagner. Without money, I cannot

continue to raise him."

"You are asking for money? But Heinrich doesn't have—"

"I want no money. For myself, I scrub houses, I am fed. But the boy here is too large, three years old, he can no longer come with me to each workplace. You must take him. You and Heinrich. He's yours now." Abruptly, she pulled the child's hand from her own.

"Mine?" The other gasped. "I am already with child."

"So I see. You will now have another for company." Rosina bent to kiss her son. "Be good, Karl. Good-bye."

Before Margaretha could catch her breath, Rosina had straightened and was striding rapidly away, with Karl looking after her, masking a sob.

For long seconds, while the boy's sobs became audible, Margaretha stood in shock. She was torn. *Mein Gott, this can't be. How did this happen? How am I to take another's child?* But then the boy's disconsolate crying tore at her. As he snuffled and gasped, Margaretha's heart broke.

Awkwardly, she leaned down. "Oh, poor child," she said. "Poor, poor boy. Come to me." With that she squatted and took the boy in her arms. "Sweet little tyke," she murmured into his hair. Above his shoulders she saw the looming trees, the darkness deep in the forest, expanding even beyond the obvious shadows. "We cannot leave you to the fearsome forest, can we? You will have a home." Against her already-full stomach she rocked him briefly.

"Oh, Karl. How shall we tell your father?"

THE FOLLOWING YEARS DID NOT GO WELL FOR Karl. Joined by a half-sister, Marie, and later a half-brother, Gustav, he was treated by Heinrich as a nuisance—or worse, a pariah.

"Be good to him," cried Margaretha from time to time, "for he is your son, too. Ignore him and he will hate you."

His answer was a stony stare. And then, "Not willingly mine, he's not. His mother brought him to taunt me—that I married you instead of her. She had other lovers."

"He looks like you."

"Bah! What does that mean, woman? I do not accept him as mine."

"But you must." Karl was now almost five.

Even as he grew older and increasingly resembled his father, the boy seemed to attract only added paternal hostility.

At last Margaretha felt she must act. Karl had now turned fourteen.

Telling no one her plan, she began earning money, often secretly, then hiding most of it. From the finer households she took in sewing. Washed her neighbor's clothes. Served as a tutor, teaching children to read. On rare nights she handed over coins to Heinrich, but kept more for herself.

Within a year and a half she had managed the price of a boat passage to America. One day when Karl was still sixteen, she secretly and quickly packed a duffel with his clothes—garments that required minimum space, since he was full grown, but only 5 feet 6 inches tall. She found them both a carriage ride to Hamburg.

With great sadness, she stood with him on the dock and quickly kissed the youth she'd so lovingly raised as her own. "Be good, Karl," she whispered to him.

It was the second time in his life he'd heard the same admonition—the second time he'd been sent away. But this time the love that accompanied him formed a comforting shield against pain, a layer that warmed him and eased his departure.

In July, 1883, listed on the ship manifest, the *Selisia,* as a "joiner," in possession of only one bag, Karl became part of New York City's untamed, uncounted masses. With what ingenuity he managed to survive, even prosper, no record remains. Was he fed through the kindness of strangers? Given a job by dint of his youth and seventeen-year-old strength? Or did he simply find within himself the needed inspiration, bestowed so recently by a determined and loving step mother?

Documents show that Karl Wagner Klumpp was naturalized on June 12, 1889, and when he applied for a passport in 1896 at the age of 29, he listed his occupation as "barber." In that 1896 application he wrote that he intended to go back to Germany and return "within one year."

Though it is not known how or where he found Marie Caroline Hayoz, eleven years his junior, surely it was a fortuitous encounter.

However they chanced to meet, one fact remains: they were married on December 5, 1897. And in time the two ran a bakery shop in the Bronx.

IN MAY OF 1903, MY FATHER WAS BORN AS THE first child of Marie Carolyn Hayoz Klumpp, a birth that was followed three years later by that of a daughter.

My dad, Theodore George Klumpp, seldom spoke to us about those growing-up years, when he and his one sister, Margaret, delivered fresh-baked bread to their parents' customers.

But for their children the parents had loftier goals than bread delivery: they managed somehow to send their son to Princeton and their daughter to Cornell.

Later I wished that somebody had recorded which parent—or was it both?—who inspired their two children to leave their humble Bronx backgrounds and enroll in two of the country's most elite universities.

BECAUSE THEODORE ENTERED PRINCETON'S

freshman class of 1924 without the customary social credentials, neither wealth nor membership in Eastern high society—and in spite of his obvious good looks—young Theodore Klumpp was never invited to join the prestigious Princeton Eating Club. Thus passed over, he said, "I'll form my own eating group," and so he did.

It was during those Princeton years that Theodore must have met my mother, Virginia Allan. When she brought him home to meet Russell, her rich father's approval was immediate. "He's graduating Magna Cum Laude," Virginia said. "And now he's been accepted to Harvard Medical school," which was all the prompting Russell needed. "Tell him to begin his medical education," said Russell. "And send the bills to me."

Thus did two amazing grandfathers converge to promote the career of one promising young man. For Russell it was an obvious decision to invest in a man whom he saw, correctly, as having a stellar future. Midway through his medical school education, according to the New York Times of February 14, 1926, Virginia Allan and Theodore Klumpp became engaged. The two were married later that year.

FOLLOWING HER BROTHER'S EXAMPLE, MARGARET Klumpp, too, applied for admission to medical school. But she was told by the dean of Cornell, "I'm sorry, Miss Klumpp. This education would be wasted on you.

You'll marry and have children and drop out. We cannot squander a classroom seat on a woman."

"But I won't drop out," she argued, "I give my word. No matter how my family life unfolds, I'll still continue my medical practice." With that promise taken at face value, she was accepted and became a dermatologist, one of the first female doctors in the United States. Keeping her word to the medical school—and in spite of an exceptionally good marriage to a businessman named Art Searing—she continued her dermatology practice for a lifetime.

Unfortunately, Margaret was unable to have children of her own, but instead she later became a loving aunt to her brother's children.

ONCE GRADUATED FROM HARVARD, DR. THEODORE Klumpp did his residency at the Peter Bent Brigham hospital in Boston, and was there when I was born. A short time later he was asked to teach medicine at Yale, and later at George Washington University.

Sadly, Karl Wagner Klumpp died in 1928, one year before his first grandchild was born. But he lived long enough to bask in the unfolding careers of his two children.

My father's teaching years ended in 1936, when he was tapped to become the chief medical officer for the Food and Drug Administration, a position he held until

1941. Passionate about the problems of aging and a strong proponent of exercise (not then a universally accepted mantra), he began writing articles on the subject, including some which were accepted by my beloved *Reader's Digest*.

Sometime during that era, after about five years of marriage, my mother divorced him. For my mother, we surmised, he fell short as a Casanova.

In 1942, Dr. Theodore George Klumpp was chosen by board members of Sterling Drug to become the CEO of Winthrop Laboratories in New York City.

With his new wife, also named Virginia, he built a home in Sands Point on Long Island which, with its astonishing views of Long Island Sound, was featured in *House Beautiful*. This was the house where, as an adult, I finally came to know my father—not as a kind of specter during a fleeting appearance on our ranch—but as a real person.

Still, that week of our first acquaintance stands out as a transformative moment in my growing up.

(This chapter was written for my memoir, *The Tail on my Mother's Kite*, but later omitted.)

Naked And Afraid—with my Nephew, Billy Berger

He was naked and cold, but his thoughts were not what he you'd think: his fears were narrow and centered on one possibility—that he might step on a water moccasin. And his daily activities, all spent with an equally naked woman, were not what you'd imagine, either. Billy Berger's focus was definitely not on romance.

After an hour talking to my nephew, whom I last saw when he was just a boy, I now have a mental picture of what it was like, this 21 days in a swamp near Baton Rouge. Frankly, I was fascinated. First, that he sounded so normal. Second, that his 21 days were so anything but normal.

Billy Berger, my nephew, was no stranger to "roughing it." Before his 2013 appearance on *Naked and Afraid*, Billy played a key role in the Discovery Channel's *I, Caveman*, which appeared in 2011.

Alone among a group of ten people attempting to live with no tools other than those available to cavemen, Billy Berger managed to use his stone tools to butcher an elk brought down by another of the group—a man who used a spear and a spear-thrower (atlatl), to fell the animal. (Earlier, Billy had thrown his spear and missed).

Between them, the two men gave the group enough meat to survive.

This was the first big game kill documented in modern times.

As the week (or weeks), progressed, a number of players dropped out. "And the funny thing was," Billy said, "you couldn't tell at the beginning who would last and who wouldn't. One of the men came into the event with a pompous attitude, as though he'd breeze through it—but he was among those who quit. A woman, Manu, was beset with enough discouraging problems to make her give up. Instead, she became an inspiration for the entire group and lasted until the end."

Among the ten was Morgan Spurlock, now an investigative journalist for CNN, who remarked at the end, "Billy, I'm glad you were with us—without you it would have been a disaster."

On the basis of that show and his own YouTube portrayals of survival skills, Berger was chosen to appear on the 21-day adventure, *Naked and Afraid*.

"What made you decide to do it?" I asked.

"I enjoy a challenge. And it might give me exposure for other jobs."

"Did you know what you were getting into?"

"No. I did it blind. Actually, I was so concerned (he wouldn't use the word "afraid"), that I spent sleepless nights worrying. None of the shows by then had ever aired. I considered dieting to get my body used to starvation, but decided against it. I realized I'd need all the body fat I could get. Instead I ate normally and kept going to the gym."

"Weren't you embarrassed—being naked?"

"Sure. For the first hour. I'm not an exhibitionist. But the awkwardness didn't last long. After an hour, we weren't thinking about our nakedness—we were trying to figure out how to survive."

"What was the worst part?"

"At first, the cold. We were in the swamps outside Baton Rouge. A cold snap came through as we began, and we were freezing. Forty-eight degrees. But it didn't help to cuddle. When you're both cold, with no blanket to keep in the heat, huddling together doesn't work. We quickly gave it up. Instead, we had to create some shelter and a fire."

"Like how? With no tools, no wood scraps. Nothing."

"Actually, I had a knife, and she had a fire starter—but that was all. I used sticks to create a framework and palmetto fronds to wrap around it, stuff I tied together with roots and vines."

"Tell me about your partner. "

"Her name was Ky Furneaux; she was an Australian who'd been a stunt woman. She was my rock. She kept me going when I became discouraged. A positive attitude was hard to maintain, but she stayed positive enough for both of us. By seven or eight days, I was so hungry that just standing up made me light-headed.

"Luckily, Ky found a discarded cooking pot, so we had a container to boil water. But we had to walk quite a way to get it, because the cameramen churned up the nearby water and made it murky. Even so, we had to boil our water for quite a while to kill the germs—and then let it cool. We were both dehydrated—so much so that my salivary glands stopped working. It was hard to swallow anything."

"What DID you eat?"

"Certain plants that I knew were safe. Whatever we could find or catch. Crawdads. And once we caught a nutria—that was the best. I was used to eating bland food—no sugar, no sodas, no candy in my normal diet, so for me this stuff didn't taste bad."

"Did anything really dramatic happen?"

"Yeah. The area had a lot more snakes than I figured—I had some close calls, when I nearly stepped on water moccasins. And three times our fire blew out, and I had to re-start it—the hard way. The fire was critical … for purifying our water, for body heat, for cooking."

"What did you get out of the experience, Billy?"

"A little money, but not much. About what I would have earned on the outside during those 21 days. And lots of exposure. Turns out our episode was the most popular of the Discovery Channel season. They played it over and over."

"But you didn't get residuals."

"No."

"Any repercussions later?"

"Oh, yes. Once back in civilization, I discovered I couldn't tolerate food with flavor. It stung my mouth— even the smallest amounts of salt or sugar. In fact a banana was too sweet. I had to stick to plain lettuce and boiled chicken. Also, thanks to the dehydration, my salivary glands were out of commission for nearly a month—so food kept sticking in my throat.

"Later I was asked to be a "peacekeeper" in three versions of the *Hunger Games*, which I did. Quite a long time after that, *Naked and Afraid* asked me to do a forty-day segment. I decided that was just too dangerous, so I turned it down."

"What about Ky? Are you still friends with her?"

"Sure. We'll always be friends. You can't go through something like that and not remain close."

Billy's episode was filmed in May, 2013, and aired on July 28, 2013. It's called, *Beware the Bayou*. You can still find his program online, *Beware the Bayou*, as filmed by the Discovery Channel.

When you talk to Billy Berger, he doesn't sound eccentric, or like anything but just a normal guy. Over the phone he makes the experience of *Naked and Afraid* sound like a perfectly reasonable thing to do.

SENTIMENTAL JOURNEY?

THREE WEEKS BEFORE FEBRUARY 14, ROB HANDED me the envelope, which clearly had a Valentine inside. The outside said, "M. On 2/14." He said, "Save it, Babe, for the right day."

That's when I knew that Rob, who doesn't plan such things in advance, hadn't spent one minute standing in an aisle somewhere, painstakingly sorting through Valentine messages. Whatever it was, somebody else had chosen the message—hopefully, in his voice. Knowing how he operates, I imagined the thing had arrived in the mail. Meaning, of course, Rob had chosen to hop aboard some passing sentiment like a hobo on a box car, traveling for free.

Still, hoping some stranger had penned words worth keeping, I propped up the card in a prominent spot and waited. On the fourteenth, I opened it.

Outside, the words were promising: "To Someone Special. On Valentine's Day." Inside, the message took a dive. "This special card is sent your way, filled with good thoughts on Valentine's Day." Rob had circled the words "good thoughts."

I stared at it, incredulous. "Good thoughts?" *Good thoughts*? Was that the best the writer could offer? Was that the best Rob could do? Good thoughts in a lousy meter?

Next to the pre-fab message, Rob had printed, "Doesn't get better than this … "

Suddenly I was laughing. Of all the intentionally funny cards I've ever received, this was one of the funniest—except it wasn't intentional. This one had gone straight from stupid to hilarious. Right there, it was Rob all over … his ever-present sense of the banal, his refusal to subscribe to "love by decree."

Which didn't do *me* any good.

After 66 years of marriage, I thought, *maybe I'd better just grab Good Thoughts and run.* For weeks afterwards one of us would say something like, "Had any Good Thoughts lately?" and we'd break up laughing.

All of which reminds me of other supposedly sentimental moments that fall flat, such as a bridegroom suddenly forgetting his bride's name. One of my best friends, Elaine, accepted a blind date, and when he arrived she opened the front door, took one look and said, "You're too short," and closed the door in his face. When she opened it again, Marty was laughing. From that moment on, their relationship soared.

It also reminds me of Rob, whose marriage proposal came after numerous trips down Bayshore Highway from his school, San Jose State, to mine—Stanford. One day he said offhandedly, "This trip has gotten so grueling, we might as well get married."

After a sideways proposal like that—which I accepted immediately—the pundits would have given us six months. They should have been right.

Except they were wrong. I didn't get the sentiment, but I got the man.

Anyway, just so you'll know, I've had better Valentines. Last year's card from the American Heart Association was a whole lot classier than this one. The heart folks will never know, but thanks to this year's remarkably clunky card, Rob owes me dinner at a fancy restaurant.

I picked The Ritz—and eventually got it!

Three Men Who Did the Seemingly Impossible

THE GASH IN HIS SHIN NEEDED STITCHES. YET JIM Klumpp was on the Appalachian Trail in New Hampshire, miles from anywhere, having just skidded off a wet, mossy rock and into a sharp tree branch. Until a fellow hiker bound up the wound, the blood poured down his leg. No car, no ambulance was anywhere close. Jim was forced to hike another two miles, injured or not, to get preliminary medical help, and then another five miles on a still-unstitched shin for real repairs.

To prevent infection, the doctor who finally saw Jim used tape instead of stitches, and advised his patient to take a week off to rest the wound. Thus, when Jim returned to the trail, his daily hike went from some twenty miles a day to a few thirty-milers, determined as he was to catch up with trail friends who were now miles ahead of him.

Jim Klumpp, age 55, is my nephew. He began his trek in Georgia, a 2,185-mile adventure that took him four and a half months. He wore out six pairs of shoes, and was left with numb feet, a temporarily crooked back, and a brief period of total exhaustion. Yet the experience, with angels appearing here and there to feed and care for him and other hikers (which he calls "trail magic") and brief encounters that turned into lasting friendships— was so exhilarating, that in spite of many days hiking alone, Jim was never sorry to be doing it.

A large number of people read Jim's daily posts. With some 150,000 hits, friends and strangers followed his story, told calmly but with an eye for fascinating detail. Jim's journal arrived weeks ago, and has now become my daily reading and given me things to be surprised about: that, except for scattered restaurant meals, Jim and fellow hikers subsisted mainly on junk food—pop tarts and Snickers bars; that his pack totaled 34 pounds, yet the stove, tent, sleeping bag, and sleeping pad, accounted for only 12 of them; that he was often wet, frequently sloshed through mud or climbed uphill over slippery rocks, that he bathed periodically in cold streams and ponds, but never found anything worth complaining about.

Google says that the full trek from Georgia to Maine is the equivalent of hiking from sea level to the top of Everest and back 16 times. But this trail experience is not Jim Klumpp's first physical adventure. At age 17, he and a friend rode bicycles from the Atlantic Ocean, across the United States to the Pacific. My final thought: Everything Jim Klumpp described as he hiked the Appalachian Trail made me supremely proud of him

... but also supremely glad to be safe and comfortable in my own home.

NAKED AND NOT AFRAID WOULD BE A BETTER TItle for the 21-day adventures of Billy Berger and his female partner, Ky Furneaux. As described in a previous blog, (*Naked and Afraid*), Billy had to find ways to survive in a Louisiana swamp with no clothing and only two implements—a knife for him and a fire-starter for her.

With great ingenuity, Billy found ways to turn plants and leaves into shelter, to collect and boil enough water to keep them both alive, and to find leaves, crawdads, and a single captured nutria as life-sustaining nourishment.

Like Jim Klumpp, Billy Berger's *Naked and Afraid* was not his first physical ordeal. A few years earlier, he was an outstanding participant in a group of ten people who tried, for the Discovery Channel show, to exist under primitive conditions, living with the same tools as existed for our ancestors—and thus that earlier show was called, *I, Caveman*.

BACK IN 1973, A YOUNG HANG GLIDING PILOT, BOBBY Wills, already a champion in the sport, found a way to set a world record as he flew continuously, with no return to earth, for eight hours and twenty-four minutes. He was on Oahu, Hawaii, soaring in what is called "ridge lift" off a thousand foot cliff near Sea Life Park. By today's standards, everything about his equipment was rudimentary; he was seated on a swing seat from Sears, his control of the glider came by manipulating a triangular aluminum bar, and his legs hung freely in space.

Occasionally, just to vary his position, Bobby climbed off the seat and wedged himself into the triangle, peering out at the world like a gibbon.

Odd as it seems, the trade wind over the ocean, blowing nonstop, became unbearably cold to someone who was sitting still and flying barefoot—with only a short-sleeve shirt. His brother, Chris, attempting to set the record with him, gave up after a few hours. Unable to endure the cold, Chris landed back on the beach.

Still, Chris recognized that even Bobby might not last without a jacket, and so Chris figured out a way to "fly" a jacket out to his brother. Over the ocean once more, he released a bundled-up jacket on a long string, and Bobby somehow flew underneath, broke the string and secured the garment.

For another five hours, Bobby flew on, literally into the sunset. His physical ordeal amazed fellow pilots and secured a place for him in world hang gliding records. The scene is described fully in my memoir, *Higher Than Eagles*.

Jim Klumpp's journal was enlivened with photos. As I read his story, I began to grasp the relationship between these three men. First, I am related to all of them. Jim and Billy are my nephews. Bobby is our son.

All three are grandsons of my father, Dr. Theodore George Klumpp, whose story is also remarkable, but wholly different. As described in an earlier chapter, his parents ran a bakery shop in the Bronx, and my father rose from delivering bread as a kid, to a medical degree from Harvard, to a stint as chief medical officer for the FDA, and then to President of Winthrop Laboratories.

I've never stopped to think about this before, but suddenly I realized the amazing truth: these three remarkable men are cousins.

Big Hearts in Texas

The high school boys in Texas' Gainesville Correctional Facility didn't get out much. They called themselves The Tornados, and they were basketball players—but it was only as a reward for good behavior that the boys were allowed to leave the facility at all, and then only to play basketball against a few private Texas schools.

It was Steve Hartman who found them *On the Road*. The Gainesville boys told him, "Our fan base was close to zero. Nobody was allowed out to see us play. Nobody saw us, really, and nobody cared."

But far away, something else was happening. Two young players from Vanguard Prep school in Waco, knew the Gainesville boys would soon be coming. Together, they grasped what seemed an unfair situation. "We aren't going to play a team," one of them said, "that has no fans and no supporters. It doesn't seem right."

With their special brand of magic, before the arrival of the Gainesville team, the two Waco players re-organized their own fans, asking that half the audience cheer for the Gainesville boys. Taking it a step further, they found five girls and outfitted them in Gainesville uniforms, preparing them to organize cheers for the other team.

As Hartman says, "That night the real game wasn't on the court: it was in the stands."

When the Gainesville team arrived to play, they had no idea that something unusual was about to happen. But from the start a surprise awaited them.

To the astonishment of the Correctional Facility boys, who hadn't seen it coming, every basket they made was accompanied by enthusiastic whoops and yells. From the sidelines, those five girls in special uniforms led cheers.

At times, their solid group of fans leaped to their feet to urge them on. The Gainesville boys were likely playing to sounds they'd never heard before. Amazed and overwhelmed, the Gainesville guys played their hearts out.

At the end, as their supporters had been doing all along, a huge section of the audience rose, clapped and cheered.

Afterwards, one of the boys told Steve Hartman, "I'll remember it for the rest of my life." Another said, "It's something I won't forget." And another, "If I live to be 70, I'll never forget this."

As Hartman summed up the night, "Nobody cared who won. So we don't care, either."

In an interview days later, the two Vanguard boys voiced their own thoughts. "This is how sports should be."

Can We Live a Lot Longer?

THE BABY APPEARED ON THE COVER OF *Time Magazine*, (February 3, 2015), with the caption: "This baby could live to be 142 years old." Since they picked the world's cutest little guy, most of us would vote to let him live indefinitely.

The article was pages and pages long, but what came through like a mantra from on high was the value of exercise. Second, perhaps, was attitude. *Time* says, "'You're only as old as you feel' may merely be part of the equation. Perhaps, within reason, you're only as old as you bloody well choose to be." The article adds, "Research is mounting that your outlook, your personality and, frankly, how upbeat you are have a profound impact, not just on how you feel but also on how your cells age."

I started this blog intent on a different aspect of health. Food. It was the baby who got me off track.

As some of you know, I'm now working on a book with breast surgeon John West. Titled, "*PREVENT! SURVIVE! THRIVE! Every Woman's Guide to Optimal Breast Care.*" Dr. West chose an early chapter to discuss the importance of lifestyle in preventing breast cancer. He too, stresses exercise and rejects sugar.

But then he quotes an astonishing 30-year study of

200,000 people … an attempt to link certain foods to longevity. Now Dr. West asks his patients, "What food do you think is most important to help you live longer?"

So here I'm asking all of you. What food to you think it is?

Like Dr. West's patients, I would have said broccoli. Also like his patients, I would have been wrong.

The answer is nuts.

Apparently, the more nuts we eat the better—and any kind will do. Furthermore, the nut eaters tended to be slimmer than everyone else. Meaning nuts are not as fattening as we think.

The minute I typed that chapter, I began starting my days with a handful of nuts and seeds. (A neat little trail mix package from Vons). I also give them to Rob. Is it my imagination that various aches and pains have subsided?

The nuts are easy. Harder for me is giving up sugar. But I'm trying. I'm trying.

I'll let you know in a few months how this all works out.

A Word that Defines Success

I first heard the word on a TV program called *TED*—which stands for Technology, Entertainment, Design. That night the topic was Education. Each speaker was given 18 minutes, but the one that impressed me most was a teacher-turned-psychologist. She and a few others like her studied schools, teachers, and students in numerous settings, trying to discover the one quality in students that made them succeed. They watched, they observed, they photographed.

And who did best?

She said it wasn't the kids whose IQs were highest. It wasn't the kids who had the greatest social skills. It wasn't the students who were the best looking.

The narrator took a deep breath and stared at the audience. "It was the kids with GRIT." Deliberately she elaborated. "We noticed the successful kids were those who persevered, who went for the marathon, not the sprint ... the kids who just kept at it, who wouldn't quit, who persisted no matter what the odds against them." The most successful students, she said, were those who were willing to take an hour and a half bus ride just to get to a better school.

She kept asking, "How do we give our kids this quality? How do we instill GRIT?"

The audience listened and stared back. It was obvious that neither she nor anybody else had the answer. How DO we inspire kids? How do we instill grit? Or does it just "come" with certain kids?

As I pondered, I was musing in a way about me, because I'm not the smartest writer out there, nor the most creative. And maybe I don't write the best books, either. But I don't quit. I don't give up. Those 14 years I was trying to get *Higher Than Eagles* published, I just kept re-writing. Over and over as I polished and re-edited familiar pages, I recited a mantra: *If I make this good enough, someone will HAVE to buy it*. I stopped counting the rejections for that book—there were just too many.

Yet in the end, when it finally attracted an editor … when it was finally published … readers and reviewers were enthusiastic, beyond what I'd ever dreamed. And the book received five movie options, including from Disney.

So this is what I told my writing students, next class. If you want to succeed in this writing game you have to push on. You don't need to be the smartest or the wittiest or the most creative—you just have to be the most determined. You must absolutely decide that you'll make it. And then you must march ahead relentlessly— re-write your work until it sparkles, search everywhere

for editors—behind obstacles and in little-known places—decide you will never give up.

In your head the operative word should never be "If."
Only "when." Eventually you'll find that you had what it
took. That all along you had GRIT.

Horror In The Cockpit

As of this morning, we know so little about that crash in the French Alps. Yet what few details have come out suggest scenarios we can hardly bear to contemplate. In fact, it seems that a lot of future aviation may be at stake.

I first heard about the accident in a strange way. My granddaughter, whose husband is currently getting his MBA in Barcelona, emailed me Tuesday morning: "Mike's professor's family was on the plane that crashed today. His school is cancelled on Friday."

I stared at her email. What plane? I wondered. What crash?

Only by backing up my e-mails did I find it—news that hours earlier a plane from Barcelona to Düsseldorf had gone down, with no survivors expected. Even the earliest reports were baffling: no pilot had radioed the tower; no distress call was ever received.

Years ago I wrote a book about airplane sabotage, a techno-thriller called *Scatterpath*. What made it fascinating to me were the revelations made by the NTSB investigator with whom I worked closely for three years. Among them was the explanation that U.S. pilots are given assertiveness training so that no co-pilot will be dominated by his superior ... that everyone in the cockpit will feel free to speak up in case of impending disaster.

In fact, the Korean plane crash in San Francisco was made worse by the failure of an Asian co-pilot (maybe two) to warn his "superior" that the plane was coming in too low. Asian culture demands that the man in charge does not allow his inferiors to overrule him. As we all learned, the plane hit a sea wall before it crash-landed.

Today's revelations were startling at first—then chilling. One of the two pilots, having left the cockpit at top cruising altitude, couldn't get back in. The voice recorder revealed that even after he knocked politely, then harder, then tried to break the door down, no answer came from inside. No voice was heard. Was the remaining pilot incapacitated? Had he locked the door accidentally? Was he unable to admit the man on the outside?

Was this truly an accident?

But tonight an expert pilot interviewed on television assured the public that all pilots have a code to punch for re-entering the cockpit. Only by continuous, energetic override from the inside, he said, could the outsider be kept out.

As of Wednesday night, this is all we know: no pilot radioed the tower. The second pilot tried and seemingly failed to get back inside his cockpit. With a probable "code" available for readmission ... what actually happened to keep him out?

As a writer, I couldn't have dreamed up such a set of bizarre circumstances—a scenario that ended so badly.

Now we all want to know: who WERE these two pilots? And what motivated one of them to refuse admittance to the other? Was the inside man really *trying* to bring down a plane?

Shortly we will probably learn a great deal more than we do now. Thank heavens for "black boxes." Which, as most of you know, are really orange.

Star Billing I Never Wanted

For a small drone, the machine kicked up a mighty wind. Six family members sat mesmerized as the plaything zoomed around my son's family room like an angry hornet, lights flashing, four propellers creating a miniature hurricane, more breeze than anyone expected.

What I *should* have expected was that eventually it would hit me. Like others in the room, I kept ducking. Then … Clunk. The spinning, futuristic toy came to a sudden stop against my upper lip. A nasty surprise. And this collision thanks to my son, Chris, who, in addition to being an excellent surgeon is reputedly a good pilot.

"But of course," my husband muttered, "it had to be you."

As Chris' wife, Betty-Jo, handed me a damp towel for the few drops of blood the drone released, I suddenly remembered. Oh, yeah … I've got this history.

Over the years I've noticed other people acquire reputations they relish. Whereas I'd like to be renowned as a writer, within my family I'm famous for being a target.

It all started innocently enough, years ago, when I stood near a railing at Brandon's ice hockey game. First grandson, first time I'd ever attended a game—and to add to my uncanny luck, other family members stood beside me. But only I was singled out by the puck that unexpectedly sailed skyward off the ice, cleared the railing and smacked my upper arm. It hurt like crazy. Still, I felt lucky. It could have been my head. It was Chris, standing next to me, who noted, "Of course, Mom, you were the one that got nailed." How he recognized this tendency so early is difficult to imagine. But let's just say his observation was predictive of future events.

Once another grandson, Dane, became fully invested in volleyball, Rob and I attended most of his matches. The Anaheim Sports Arena contains some twenty volleyball courts. Unlike other spectators, I've been hit by balls flying out of at least ten of them. Balls from courts behind me clunk against the net and find my back. Balls from warm-up smashes in front of me career off my forehead. Balls from near-empty courts seek me out as I head for the cafeteria—and one managed to knock off my glasses.

For that matter, my glasses alone have taken hits and flown off my face at least three times.

Other spectators began to notice. "You do seem to have a bulls eye painted on your body," a team mother said. Her husband added, "You know, Maralys, you really need to wear a helmet." Another mother said, "Don't sit by her—she gets hit every time."

Once, in the Anaheim arena, as I was headed for

the ladies room, a ball from a nearby court followed me down a narrow hall and brushed me as I entered the restroom.

The most spectacular moment actually occurred in a high school gymnasium. Like other spectators, I was sitting quietly in the bleachers when it happened. A volleyball from the court in front of us sailed down the length of the gymnasium, hit a wall at the far end and rebounded, flying like a homing pigeon straight for my head. Dozens of other heads were available, of course, but obviously mine was the only one with a ball-attracting magnet.

My family finds all this amusing, as though it's somehow my fault. They weren't surprised when we were walking together across a soccer field and an errant ball from a distant kick found me and bounced off my ankle. But even our guffawing males didn't witness the ultimate in heat-seeking missiles.

That came when, with my granddaughter Christy up in Oakland, I visited a tiny tots birthday party. Like grasshoppers, some dozen three-year-olds cavorted and frolicked across a modest living room, chasing small toys and piñata candies. Among the objects on the floor was a tiny ball. To my astonishment, a miniature boy took a mighty swing with his miniature toe, caught the ball just right, and sent it cascading into my cheek.

The father sitting beside me exclaimed, "Oh! Are

you all right?"

He probably didn't believe me when I said, "Well, that was certainly the smallest of my assailants. You wouldn't know this, of course, but I'm famous for getting hit by flying balls. In fact, I'm verging on a national reputation."

We both laughed.

At the time I thought the little boy had achieved top billing. But that was before Chris brought home a drone. While I admire him as a pilot, when it comes to his expertise with this simplest of toys, my admiration dwindles and I'd rather be elsewhere. I don't need my son adding another hash-mark to my considerable renown as a target.

A Passion Worth Millions

I FIRST SAW HIM ON *SIXTY MINUTES*—LAWYER Bryan Stevenson in an abbreviated version of his appearance on the TV program, *TED*. It seems that Stevenson's 18-minute talk on legal injustice inspired *TED* viewers to contribute over a million dollars to his Equal Justice Initiative. Yet Stevenson's talk was not a plea for money—it was a spirited description of legal inequality in America, especially among blacks. He said, "The opposite of poverty is not wealth. It's justice."

Stevenson's appearance on *TED* was no accident. One of the producers said, "If we're thinking about doing a story on somebody, we talk to them, and we try to look at a video of them to see if they have passion." As the show evolved, the producers realized that yes ... they wanted the personal stories—PLUS the big idea.

Passion is obvious in Lincoln's words at Gettysburg, when he speaks of "a new nation, conceived in liberty, and dedicated to the proposition that all men are created equal," or Jack Kennedy's plea for Americans to, "Ask not what your country can do for you, ask what you can do for your country," or Martin Luther King's "I have a dream," all words replayed constantly.

But think of THIS YEAR—when Dan Price,

owner of Gravity Payments in Seattle, spoke about the ongoing passion of his employees ... and how, after sleepless nights, he decided to reduce his own salary by 90 percent and the company profits, too, so he could significantly raise all the employee salaries. His decision made a new kind of history. But more important, it brought Dan Price a special kind of happiness. He has since heard from 100 other CEOs who applaud his move.

Or consider Nick Hanauer, among the richest businessmen in America, who said, "The pitchforks are coming ... The idiotic trickle-down policies are destroying my customer base ... When workers have more money, businesses have more customers." On the back of his beliefs, he campaigned for a $15.00 minimum wage in Washington State. To his amazement, a year later it happened.

My intention was to write about what happens when I'm passionate. Here is a story so mundane it shouldn't be included, but I'll tell it anyway. I've gotten only three traffic tickets in my life. Each time I believed I was right and the policeman was wrong. (This is not to say I've never deserved a ticket. I have. Just not these.)

Each time, I went to court to plead my case. As I sat watching other drivers turned down by the judge at hand, I wondered why I'd made the effort. Yet three times I believed so strongly in my own circumstances that the judge ruled in my favor. And each time, the policeman was sitting right there.

Over the years, passion has served me well. But this riff isn't about me. It's about how, in the end, passion carries the day. If you REALLY care about something, tell others. Speak up. Tell the world. One passionate person is worth a thousand who don't care enough to utter a peep.

Your Sock Is Dead and Buried

Over the years I've tried to explain this to my kids—or worse, to my lawyer husband. "I hate to tell you this, but your other sock is nowhere. It's gone."

"You're in charge here," says my husband. "Socks don't just evaporate. So where is it?"

"If I knew, Rob, I'd give it to you. But I don't have the slightest idea. It went into the laundry … and I guess it died, because it never came out."

I get this shaking of the head and this look—an irritated frown that suggests I'm crazy. But if I'm nuts, so is every woman I've ever known. Socks disappear. It's a rule of American households. You start with a pair, and before long you've got only one. And if the missing sock ever turns up (like maybe it's been hiding under a tee-shirt nobody ever wears), by then you've thrown away its mate. So you've still got only one.

Inexplicably, the subject came up last week in my writing class—how socks enter the washing cycle and are never seen again. When you finally get around to pairing them up, about a fourth are missing. And how men can't accept it, so it must be something their wives are doing. And how any guy smarter than a pinhead knows an object as tangible as a piece of footwear doesn't just vanish.

As my student Marcia told a few of us, "My husband was dumbfounded. 'You just lost them, that's all. They have to be somewhere.'"

To which she replied, "Then you do the laundry, Tom," so for a year, he did. After a while, as the problem continued, his manly common sense reared up. "They must be in the dryer vent. They've gotta be piled up there in one big lump." With that he painstakingly took the vent apart ... and found nothing.

Next he went outside. "They must have blown right through." He examined the ground around the external opening, but all he found was traces of lint clinging to a bush.

After a year he said, "I give up, Marcia.. You take over the laundry." In her household, the mysterious issue was never raised again.

For years we've had the discussion in our house. Five boys here, lots of laundry. No lawyer would ever accept a fact not in evidence—that our dryer, in particular, harbored some kind of sock-eating demon.

No, no. Clearly the fault was mine. Over a decade, I dutifully spent some thousand hours trying to pair up socks that didn't match, ending with several dozen that didn't belong to each other, or to any sock-like close relative.

I kept those orphans all through my thirties, literally hanging on to a thread of hope. Next I bought blue for Bobby, red for Chris, and so on—meaning the left-overs were all in different colors. Finally, in desperation, I splurged—on four dozen pair, all alike, all the same shade of blue. The boys no longer had a choice. From then on, no matter what happened, I was only off by one.

Other mothers handled this differently. Dorsey labeled her daughter's socks to match her daughter's names. "A" for Audra, "B" for Bonnie, and so on. The "C" child invariably cried out, "This sock has a "B."

The problem was never solved—not for me, not for anyone. It only goes away when the children move out.

In the Wills household, however, the sock problem has become immortalized. This may seem hard to believe, but on the cover of my book, *A Circus Without Elephants*, the whole family is sitting on our roof. Even after the book was published, one detail totally escaped me—until my son, Kenny, pointed it out. "Did you ever notice, Mom, that I'm wearing two different socks?"

A Parent by Any Other Name …

It was an awful scene. So bad that my husband will be appalled that I'm even telling it. The whole family would rather I say nothing. In some ways, every respectable family lives partly in the shadows, but reveals to the world only its sunny side. No Christmas letter ever mentions that one of their kids is in jail.

And yet the scene will be forever fixed in my head. Rob and I sitting quietly in our family room chairs as our son slowly, methodically, stuffs irrelevant foods into a back pack, preparing to go out on the street. But not in any ordinary way. He'll be leaving on a bicycle. At midnight. His backpack will hang heavy from his shoulders, and never mind that he's so crippled from a recent, eight-mile walk home from jail at 4:00 a.m., that he can hardly stagger around the house—he'll ride that bike to … wherever.

"You won't take me," he says, looming over my chair. "I know you won't do it," meaning drop him off at some late-night joint to … do what? "It's all because," he says, "I have nothing. No car. No wife. No job. Nothing. I want a wife. I want kids. I'll be seventy-four when my kid is twenty." He pauses. "I want to go out and meet someone."

But not like this, I'm thinking. *Never like this.* I start to say it, but Rob shakes his head.

Kirk goes on. "Tomorrow I'll be at Cooper Street Fellowship, where I can't go anywhere for thirty days." He looks at us in despair and keeps packing.

I finally speak up. "Kirk, we have a friend who gives a speech. He says, 'What if I promised I'd give you ten million dollars if you'll take a gun with one bullet and five empty chambers and point the gun at your head and fire once. Would you do it? For ten million?'" I look hard at Kirk. "That's what you're doing. You've been drinking. You're taking a chance the cops won't pick you up. One chance out of six."

Rob gestures me to be quiet, knowing I accomplish nothing, only rile up our son.

But Kirk simply shrugs. I'm not sure he even got the point. Later I say to Rob, "He's taking the shot—but nobody's offering him ten million."

So we sit. And watch. And wish he'd sober up … while he's taking an hour to fumble and change his mind and pull from the backpack a jar that's too big … and slowly stuff in M&Ms, potato chips, two cans of V-8 juice, three-pairs of socks, a toothbrush—and, if he can find it in there somewhere, his ID and bus pass.

We can't stop him, we can only infuriate him; still, we hope that by staying calm, by pretending we're psychologists, we'll bring him to his senses. Yet we can't. A parent by any other name is still a parent.

While Kirk is yet there, driving us crazy, I'm thinking how Rob just wrote an essay that ultimately concerns our no-solution son ... how years ago Ronald Reagan closed all the mental health facilities, how people like Kirk have nowhere to go except hospitals, jail, the street, or the morgue.

Jails are not mental health facilities. Over the years, drugs and alcohol—and yes, incarceration itself—have taken a toll on him that no prison comes close to fixing. A jail by any other name is still a jail.

At last Kirk leaves ... and I look at him hard as he shrugs into his backpack, wondering if this will be my last look ... thinking how, years ago, I regretted that I never took a last look at our son Eric who left one Saturday to fly a hang glider, and who, it turned out, never came back. *This time, God help me, I'm taking a last look.*

So now it's the next morning. Rob and I haven't seen Kirk, don't know when we'll see him next, or where.

Much too early, I woke up this morning with an odd phrase inexplicably running through my head: Death by any other name ...

Kirk did not die. He returned eventually, late morning, more exhausted than ever. But willing, for the moment, to remain sober and let us take him to Cooper Fellowship. Thus our life with him slides back into familiar grooves ... of alternating desperation and hope. I'm reminded of the oft-repeated mantra of Nancy, a friend who's in the business of dealing with addicts. "As long as he's warm and breathing," she says, "there's always hope."

Too Damn Busy ... Oh, Yes!

Our kitchen floor is dirty again.

Papers are piled on my upstairs chairs.

The dry laundry is still in the dryer.

And here I am, upstairs writing.

In a few months, I muse, nobody will care that on a certain Monday the linoleum should have been swept, because by then it will be dirty again.

The important news is, I'm a grandmother with too much to do.

Too much to do is the mantra of my current life — meaning I'm luckier than I deserve, luckier than grandmothers of the last century. There's this medical book I'm writing with a doctor ... manuscripts to read and a class to teach ... four speeches coming up soon. And friends, kids, grandkids, and even great grandkids with fascinating lives, all of them sending tidbits our way—photos of a little boy's first wobbly steps, videos of a small girl's first hesitant words read from a book—details that are vivid, never boring.

What could be better, when you're my age, than a hundred reasons to get out of bed?

Each morning I briefly rationalize: If I write this story, I'll have something to keep.

Something tangible. But so will others—meaning whoever cares to read it. All these scenes committed to paper ... well hey, paper lasts, it's permanent. Short of a house fire, paper is alive forever.

Along with Too Damn Busy comes Too Many Interruptions. But what's not to like? What's more valuable than a lively pause to chat with someone you care about? However much time it consumes, it's worth those non-writing minutes.

Meanwhile, some mundane chores are still waiting, grumpy but silent. Eventually I'll sweep the kitchen floor—but does anybody really care?

I'm Smarter Than A Cat

UNTIL TODAY I WASN'T. BUT WE'LL GET TO THAT …

Remember when Jay Leno used to do his "man on the street" interviews? And some guy on the sidewalk wasn't quite sure who was Vice President of the United States? Or where he might find Antonin Scalia? It's a wonder he knew how to find his way home.

Or worse, Leno enlisted college students for make-believe quiz shows. And nobody recognized the newsworthy faces, except for a giggly girl who thought she'd seen Jimmy Carter on a ten-dollar bill …

Leno knew what he was doing: in a few brief scenes he made a million viewers feel smarter than Einstein.

Leno should have stopped by our house. For too long, the order of smartness, bottom up, was me, Rob, and the cat. The brightest among us had an unpleasant habit of sneaking into the living room, where he sharpened his nails on, what else? … The nicest chair in the house. Like Leno, Pretty Boy knew what he was doing—only the best was good enough for those razor-sharp claws. Nicely sharpened, they helped propel him onto the highest beams in our breakfast room, structures Rob and I wouldn't be able to reach with a cherry-picker.

Finally we'd had enough. Or rather, our fraying chair

had had enough. Since Pretty Boy had figured out how to pry open the sliding door that leads to the living room, Rob installed a hook and eye, which we kept locked, especially at night. Yet some mornings I came out to find the door cracked, with a cat-like space leering at me.

"Did you unhook the door?" I asked Rob.

"No," he said. "I didn't. Last night, did you remember to lock it?"

"Well ... I think I did."

That incriminating space was giving me a complex, making me imagine I might have Alzheimer's. Did I really forget to lock the door?

Then one early morning I happened to be on the living room side when I saw the locked door begin to move. It wobbled and trembled, until a tiny space opened up—and then, here came the cat. Darned if he hadn't learned how to paw and jiggle the door until at last the hook flew up and out of the eye.

Oh thank heavens, I thought. *All along it was him, not me.*

"I'll have to install a stronger hook and eye," said Rob.

No longer fearing I might be dim-witted, I said, "Please do, Rob. Now."

Then something occurred to me. Maybe I ought to hook the door, but leave it slightly ajar—right to the end of the hook. Clearly, the cat could only push in one direction. Even he, Nasty Genius, couldn't make it wiggle and go the other way. I stared at the door. "Son of a gun, Pretty Boy, I'm leaving you no jiggle room."

That night I did it my way. And halleluiah! Next morning the door was still latched, and the space I'd created was still there, but too narrow for a cat.

Rob was kind enough to note my brilliance and congratulate me. At the very least I'd saved him some carpentry. And while neither of us suggests I'm brighter than he is, at least he agrees—I'm smarter than the cat.

Not Another Password … !

It happened again today. The breast care doctor with whom I'm writing a book sent me a message I couldn't open. His three important sentences were buried in password perdition—deep enough to require that I reply with a second email, requesting permission to create a password so I could open the first email.

Somebody out there must be watching our smallest, slightest moves—like every word we type. You'd think we were sharing atomic secrets.

The password plague has spread like the breast cancer we're writing about. Once it was kind of casual—you picked a few words that were easy to remember, and once every six months you might have to use them. Now the malignancy is everywhere, taking over our very bones. To use the bathroom at CVS pharmacy, you have to type in a code. Which is galling … that here, and I suppose soon everywhere, you need a password to pee.

My aversion to mindless secrecy goes way back—I mean, way, way back. As a teenager I unwittingly became a member of what was called Rainbow Girls, a desperately clandestine organization whose secrets were so tightly held we were forbidden to share them with anyone under … well, under penalty of expulsion.

202

Most of what they talked about was dull—not something I could recall until the next day. I remember thinking, *These secrets are so boring you'd have to handcuff your victim to a chair, just to get him to listen.*

For my doctor son, the password disease has spread like an epidemic—the written version of Ebola. To satisfy the requirements of the hospital, he and his colleagues are forced to change their passwords EVERY MONTH. Of course nobody short of Einstein could keep track, mentally, of twelve password changes in twelve months, so the doctors are forced to maintain written records which begin to look like the *Encyclopedia Britannica.* Once down on paper, of course, the information is "out there"—subject to misplacement, spying, or outright pilferage, thus defeating the whole purpose.

Our society is reaching some kind of tipping point, where you'll eventually need a password to open your refrigerator. Already, in one American household, at least, there's a level of secrecy none of us can quite believe. Yet it exists. In at least one home belonging to Elon Musk, you can't go from one room to another without providing a scan of your fingerprints. Really. I've often wondered— *what if you have a bathroom emergency?*

I dare not reveal her name, but one of our relatives actually worked there. Someone else, a man who ought to know, commented "This is what you'd expect from a drug dealer!"

Help! I'm A Prisoner of Publisher's Clearing House!

OKAY, I'M A SUCKER, READY TO BE EXPLOITED, I know that already. I also know there's one of me born every minute.

Somehow I drifted into this PCH prison months ago, when Publisher's Clearing House first offered to put Rob on their list of possible winners—you know, the roster that promises *somebody* will soon win $5000 a week for life, and it might as well be *him*. When I first signed up, "soon" was touted as the end of June. Yes—last month. The date has now been extended to end-of-August.

I never should have read their literature—never should have given them the slightest nod. Most important, I NEVER should have shared my email address.

Since that moment when I became a passing flake, my inbox has been bombarded with two to four messages every day, which vary from bright, golden promises "Just press this button and you'll be forever on the list—don't you WANT $5000 a week?" To threats—"If you don't sign in NOW, you'll forfeit every chance …" and I find myself thinking, "Well, I've come this far …"

Any jail house crew would call this the "good cop,

bad cop" approach, which seems to work fairly well with criminals and … well, me.

Oh, they use it, all right. But nothing is as simple as pressing a single button.

Once tapped into their site, you're bombarded with bells and kaleidoscopes and moving images, and "winning" numbers, and music, and then a continuous parade of bargain merchandise, a list that, if scrolled on paper, would reach from my second floor office down to the basement (if we had one), a list you can't get out of until you've viewed each and every item—or alternatively, turned off your computer.

Most days I bravely ignore PCH … until finally an irresistible message arrives, and once again I press a button and walk where only fools would dare to tread. And once more I put myself on a merry-go-round from which there's no escape.

But here's the amazing part—this isn't just crappy merchandise.

Among the "stuff" are dozens of household items I'd like to own … and more than that, hundreds of merchandisers who are so respectable you can't imagine why they'd stoop to advertising on Publisher's Clearing House. *Time Magazine.* The fancy Atholl Palace Hotel (already booked by us in Scotland), every insurance company, every magazine, every household item, every gadget, every business service you've ever heard of. Like me, PCH has roped them all in.

How did they do it? How does it happen that their list gets longer every day—and yes ... more respectable?

As the days went on, I could see the initial idea had morphed into something bigger. PCH realized they had to keep us pigeons going, had to keep tempting us to buy something (or lots of somethings), had to keep harvesting those millions of dollars in sales ... a tactic which is now heading in the direction of ending months from now—long past August.

When you think a little deeper, the answer is simple: as we all know, there's a sucker born every minute. But a whole lot of them happen to own businesses.

Out-Trumping Donald Trump

Donald Trump is a "Jackass."

At least that's what Senator Lindsey Graham called him, according to a recent *Los Angeles Times*.

REALLY! How fascinating that Graham saw such a different image beneath the forward-leaning hair ... but Graham ought to know, he's from South Carolina, and maybe he's seen other donkeys with a back-comb.

Whatever ... Trump is currently number one in the polls, and for some of us it's because we can't wait to hear what he'll say next—which insult he'll hurl, or where it will land. Years ago he was simply "The Donald," and he was basically a caricature you could cluck over and ignore. Now lots of voters are hoping he'll hang in for most of the electoral season, because politics is seldom this out-of-control or this funny ... and here's this one-man wrecking crew, wildly swinging away at half the politicians in his own party.

But Trump can't claim full ownership to "startling and shocking." Other luminaries are shocking, too, only some are tragically unfunny, like Bill Cosby. Few of us can imagine that this once-paragon of family values and personal ethics has now been turned over and exposed, like a rock with bugs on the other side. *Bill Cosby?* Really?

I'd be more stunned over both of them—if I hadn't personally known a couple of men who were also startling and shocking but, like Bill Cosby, were one hundred percent not the person I'd always believed.

I actually co-authored a book with a man who once stood out in my mind as the soul of ethics. The first time we met (in a restaurant, over breakfast), he took a couple of moments to pray quietly over his meal. We talked about his son and how he'd like to write a book about fatherhood. We discussed the failings of today's prison systems, and why a different approach would "rescue" and "rehabilitate" young men locked up for their addictions. We decided, informally, to write a book on the topic. We agreed to collaborate, we shook hands, and that was it. We never felt we needed a written contract.

After the book came out, this man and I traveled to other counties in his official car—to TV appearances and radio shows. We discussed ethics most of the way.

Newly elected to a high office, he was adored—first locally and then nationally. And suddenly it all fell, like a brick wall shaken to earth in a quake. He began to be discredited. The *Los Angeles Times* called me to refute certain parts of our book, which I wouldn't do; I believed he'd told the truth as he saw it. Rumors appeared in the *Times*. Friends reported to me absolute knowledge of an affair—which I found hard to believe.

It got worse. He tried to "pick up" one of my

writer-friends. Then it developed that the man's closest two buddies were both crooks. Eventually *he* was tried as a crook—with so many misdeeds on the docket that only the statue of limitations saved him from a very long prison sentence. He did, however, serve four years.

I was stunned. Who was he, anyway? The man I once knew? Or somebody else, somebody entirely different?

A second man that Rob and I knew well for over fifty years, became, after death, a complete stranger. He was once a neighbor and, with his wife, a couple we saw frequently. He was also a respected local attorney ... and in fact at one time he was president of the state bar. Both Rob and I found his sense of humor engaging.

Then the pair moved to the beach area, and we didn't see them much. Yet after he retired, the lawyer spent time in a trailer in the desert, working on a fascinating novel, for which I did some editing.

During this interval we heard a sad story about him traveling alone in Turkey, and how he woke up one morning to find himself tossed into a ditch. We were surprised at both the strangeness and his bad luck.

Then, after a long dry spell, the four of us met at Soup Plantation for lunch. It was exactly like old times. The lawyer's great sense of humor surfaced, and so did Rob's, and the four of us spent about two hours reminiscing and laughing. Nearby, a lady leaned closer and said, "It's good to see four people having so much fun."

For Rob and me, that lunch was memorable as an interval that proved old friends could still enjoy as much hilarity together as they'd once had.

Exactly four days later we received a shocking phone call—the wife reporting, in a voice thick with tears, that her husband was dead. We soon learned that a vagrant out in the desert had entered his trailer and killed him.

But this wasn't even a start to the story. Gradually it came out that the attorney had spent time in the desert for more than writing—that he'd employed a pimp to bring him ... well, male sex partners. That fatal day our friend did something that so enraged his latest conquest that the man killed him.

We never saw the wife again ... and never learned whether she was told the truth. Both Rob and I had a hard time believing there could be a side to our friend that was kept entirely secret—unknown to any of us until after his death.

The short conclusion here is that a few individuals are capable of being two entirely different people, and you never know for sure which one was "real." Every new revelation about yet another such person comes as a shock ... until the group gets so large, with so many people out-trumping Donald Trump, you're not flabbergasted any more.

And then there's The Donald himself … the one man who can never totally surprise anyone.

Why so Many Doctors Are Quitting

First it was the HMOs. Now it's the Nerds.

Thanks to nerds who write computer programs for doctors without consulting doctors—and thanks to a government that insists all medical records be electronic—today's medicine is a mess. Instead of treating patients, doctors spend patient-time staring at computers. In some programs physicians can't, for instance, refer to the term "blood." The nerds have decided the operative word for blood should be *ostag*.

Computer systems written by techs with no medical input have created an expensive, frustrating electronic hodgepodge ... in which computers from one doctor's office can't speak to those in another's, in which hospitals can't communicate with other hospitals, in which record-keeping in every doctor's office is currently like dealing with an ever-growing but insane octopus.

Diagnosis codes, for instance, have expanded from 40,000 to a little over half a million—with huge penalties if the systems aren't implemented. It's so bad now that one or two-doctor offices can no longer exist. Doctors must practice in groups, because they need several people full time just to keep the octopus under control.

Did you know that most hospitals require their doctors to create a new password every month? Tell me … who can keep track, mentally, of twelve different passwords a year? Inevitably, doctors have to write them down. Which defeats the whole idea.

I'm not a doctor, but I'm surrounded by them. One is my son, four are good friends, and another is a breast-care surgeon with whom I'm writing a book. Lately I've been thinking that America's doctors—if they weren't so busy—should rise up and revolt.

Somebody has to straighten out this mess.

If doctors were businessmen instead of doctors, the chaos would soon be gone. Think of aviation: when a pilot speaks to a control tower, every pilot in the world uses the same language—English. And every pilot communicates with the same alphabet: Alpha, Bravo, Charlie, Delta, Echo, Foxtrot …

Think of the movies—when "color" first came out, all filmmakers began using the same technology.

And remember when Beta Max promised to be the sole means of recording TV programs? But then VCR came along and took over. Later, as a group, we moved over to DVD. But at least we're all using the same system.

The problem is, good doctors want to practice medicine. Most are in the business because they care about people. They want to communicate with patients, not computers. If they MUST deal with computers, physicians want them to make sense. Today, few electronic medical systems make any sense at all … they merely waste time. So some very good doctors are giving up.

If enough doctors quit medicine, something good will definitely happen. Wait and see. There'll be a day when nobody will hire a computer nerd unless he's also a doctor.

How My Students Kept Me
from Teaching

THE SEMESTER STARTED OFF BAD AND NEVER GOT any better.

Each evening as they piled into class, one student, then another, dropped a ten-page manuscript on my desk and turned to write his name and submission title on the board. In dismay, I'd see the names and manuscripts pile up. Two or three at first, but by the time we were underway, there'd be eight to ten. And one day—eleven! I kept stealing looks at the board, knowing I'd been committed to tons of work at home. More than a hundred pages of line-by-line editing.

I pretended to like it, but I didn't. Eleven manuscripts to read on my stationary bike. But worse, another class session coming up with no time to teach.

In prior years I'd known our absolute limit was five or six manuscripts—leaving most of an hour for concentrated, hard-core lecturing. *Hey*, I'd be thinking, *I've been at this for years, and there's so much I need to tell them.* When my sessions threatened to spill over with too many manuscripts, I limited the number they could bring to class. I imagined I was doing a terrific job.

But this year I got careless, let the students write all they wanted. And now I was paying the price.

Funny thing, though—I began noticing a few students were writing better. And soon, without letting the thought filter through and become "Geronimo!" I began seeing they were ALL writing better. Every darn one of them. In class each week, we discussed what they'd created, and I had the fun of pointing out some unique, amazing, or even great lines. And then great scenes. Or I found mistakes, and instead of offering all the corrections myself, I made *them* suggest changes.

We discussed what they'd once done wrong ... and how the "wrongs" were now going away.

I never felt I was "teaching." I was always just "going over manuscripts." And while in prior years, the manuscripts diminished in number as the semester progressed, this year there was no letup. My students, darn their eyes, simply wouldn't stop writing!

On the last day I mentioned my regrets to one of my favorite students. "You know," I said, "this semester I never found time to teach."

Bridget looked at me in surprise. "Well, you didn't lecture much. But those were just words—and I'm not sure they all sank in." She paused. "We learned more by studying other manuscripts and figuring out what was wrong. And then hearing your comments and the changes you offered—or let us offer." She paused again.

"Haven't you noticed we all got better?"

"Well, actually, I did. But … there weren't any lessons. No real lessons at all."

"What do you think 'getting better' means?" She looked at me, letting it percolate. "This was one of the best semesters we've ever had."

"Really?"

"Oh, yes," she said.

I walked away with one of those cartoon light bulbs floating over my head. Before I got to the car I was thinking, *Well, hot damn, how did this happen without my noticing? All these students improving and me fussing about no time to teach.*

My husband had come this last night, and now the car was moving, but I was hardly aware of it. While he drove, I began smiling to myself.

Bridget knew it and I didn't. I must have been teaching after all.

Optimists, Take Heart!

Some Things Are Getting Better!

I WAS IN THE SAN FERNANDO VALLEY, 101 FREEWAY, when it struck me: here I am, stuck in a sea of cars, and the air is bright and clear—no smog and no cars belching fumes. In fact, not a Smoky Pierre in sight.

Years ago, the air would have been dark orange, virtually unbreathable. Without fanfare, Detroit silently cooperated with the once-denigrated air quality controllers, who persuaded engineers to create cars without toxic emissions. Ta da! … Suddenly we could all breathe again.

While they were at it, automotive geniuses improved lights, brakes, and miles per gallon, so we drivers now slurp up half the gasoline of yesterday. My old Cad from years ago got 14 MPG. A newer, hybrid Lexus SUV achieved 23 miles to the gallon. Today my Prius V gets 39 and Rob's 43—and it's no longer news.

Look at our local buses—all running smog-less on compressed natural gas.

Remember the days when your airplane's

atmosphere was polluted by cigarette smoke and you couldn't entertain at home without ash trays? And restaurants and sports events left you with hair and clothes smelling like a honky-tonk?

Who ponders this anymore? Mostly no one. Because we seldom see any smokers.

Los Angeles Times columnist, Sandy Banks, reports another victory: 300 Americans imprisoned for crimes they didn't commit have now been freed—thanks to DNA. Unlike fingerprints and eyewitness testimony, DNA is reliable.

Rob will violently disagree with this, and so will a lot of you, but I'm secretly glad that Congress is hitting investors with stealth taxes. People with money were never paying their fair share. And now, without fanfare, more of us are.

Thank heavens for iPhones with cameras ... and those photos of a few savage policemen. The public now has evidence about brutality it never found reason to stop—because few of us knew it existed. Now, with cameras everywhere, the occasional sadist in law enforcement can no longer hide.

How many of you knew that California now gets 25 percent of its energy from non-fossil-fuel sources? For starters, our own rooftop solar panels provide monthly gifts—electricity for free. These days anyone driving in the desert will see wind generators and solar panels sprouting everywhere, like flowers … and it's only getting better.

And how about newscasters who believe their viewers relish good news? Two stations now end their broadcasts on a positive note: *People Making a Difference*, and Steve Hartman's *On the Road*.

One last thing: When, thirty years ago, did you ever see a father and son hugging each other? Or for that matter, any other two men? Surely these guys have made the world a better place.

THE END

IF YOU ENJOYED THIS BOOK, I'D APPRECIATE A short review on Amazon or Goodreads. Even a few sentences will help. Reviews make all the difference in how many people will ultimately read the book.

Acknowledgements

Books don't just "happen." For most of us, books are written because something or someone inspired us to write it.

Here is a book that came about because of hundreds of faithful readers. For a number of years, people I know and a lot that I don't know, have been reading the stories posted in my blog, *A Moment With Maralys*.

Each time I put up a new one, there's an interval of excitement—those moments when I rush to the computer to find out how many people have read the new posting ... this hour, or this day. I'm always amazed that a few readers manage to appear within minutes. How did they find out so quickly? Will this be the story that goes big?

In some ways blogging is like a popularity contest, except that it's you pitted against yourself: will this subject prove more interesting than the last one? Is this the topic that will draw the greatest number of readers? Would I have done better with a different title?

My thanks go to Sue Campbell, book designer extraordinaire, whose expertise, wisdom, and timely advice played a huge role in the creation of the book.

As always, it's my husband Rob who deserves the

greatest thanks. Since I first became an author, it's been Rob who made my books possible, who gave me the unvarying support that a writer needs. Without someone to take care of the "plantation," to handle finances, to "forgive" dinner and instead take me someplace at supper time, I couldn't have squeezed out the hours that writing takes. The longer I live with Rob, the more I appreciate him.

MARALYS WILLS HAS LIVED THREE DIFFERENT lives: Mother of six children, teacher of novel-writing and memoirs, and author of sixteen books.

After six years of frequent contributions to her blog, *A Moment With Maralys*, she decided the stories needed to be collected in one spot. Hence, this volume.

Maralys enjoys speaking to groups like AAUW,

PEO, library patrons, writer's groups, and particularly book clubs. She considers interacting with an audience her dessert for all the hard work of writing.

Contact her at: Maralys@Cox.net, or (714) 544-0344.

www.ingramcontent.com/pod-product-compliance
Lightning Source LLC
LaVergne TN
LVHW051507080426
835509LV00017B/1956